TESTING THE CLAIMS OF CHURCH GROWTH

TESTING THE CLAIMS
OF CHURCH GROWTH

RODNEY E. ZWONITZER

CONCORDIA PUBLISHING HOUSE · SAINT LOUIS

*For all those saints, militant and triumphant,
who spoke the pure Gospel of Christ crucified to me.
Especially for my beloved grandmother, Sophie Zwonitzer,
who spoke the love of Christ to me so clearly
through her life and words and gifts.*

Copyright © 2002 by Rodney E. Zwonitzer
Published by Concordia Publishing House
3558 S. Jefferson Avenue, St. Louis, MO 63118-3968
Manufactured in the United States of America

Library of Congress Cataloging-in-Publication Data

Zwonitzer, Rodney E.
    Testing the claims of church growth / Rodney E. Zwonitzer.
      p. cm.
    ISBN 0-570-03324-1
    1. Church growth—Lutheran Church—Missouri Synod. 2. Lutheran Church
—Missouri Synod—Doctrines. I. Title.
    BX8061.M7 Z84 2002
254'.5—dc21

                                    2002008791

2 3 4 5 6 7 8 9 10   11 10 09 08 07 06 05 04 03

CONTENTS

PREFACE

For 13 years my life was spent in intense conference with other business executives, pondering this question: what can be done to gain more sales and/or more profit? This is what business boils down to in its most basic form. That was my venue from 1971 to 1984, advising and leading corporations such as Westinghouse, Storage Technology, and United Technologies Mostek to help market products and services with one single purpose: to gain more market share. My work consisted of segmentation analysis, product and consumer research, and the writing of marketing plans. Such plans ask, "Where have we been, where are we now, where do we want to go, and how do we get there?" Marketing exists and thrives on such plans. Most of my career was in product marketing. Here one manages a revenue stream of products. My responsibilities were to research, plan, and manage so as to maximize sales and profits. I had to determine what the product line would consist of, how it would be priced, how it would be sold to customers, and how it would be advertised. Marketing people refer to this as the "Four Ps" of marketing: product, price, place, and promotion.

In the early 1980s a sequence of events happened in my life that convinced me of God's call to prepare myself to become a pastor in His church. Many encouraged me in this endeavor. Especially did I hear how important it was that an executive with marketing expertise should become a pastor—just what the church needs, I heard and still hear many laypeople say.

But eventually, as I entered the intense study of Holy Scripture, I began to question just how much of this marketing experience should transfer over to Christ's church. I must admit that for a long period I hoped it would, since I could truly contribute the fruits of 13 years of labor out there in the business arena competing for market share. I felt this gift of talents and time would be used by God, and I was ready to share it if He wanted.

Now, on the basis of my study of Scripture, I do not believe that God wants or needs much of what I did as a marketing executive to carry over into His church. Much of the talk in our Synod these days sounds like discussions I heard in corporate conference rooms. How can we get more people interested in the faith? How can we keep them interested? How can we make them "contagious witnesses," so they reach out to others? We're losing market share. What we have been doing just doesn't work anymore. The customers just don't like it—especially those who won't be attracted to any church and those who have fallen away from attending. We must change. We must utilize all disciplines—marketing, sociology, leadership, and so forth. As a pastor and ex-marketer, I'm skeptical of this approach.

Which brings us to this book. I didn't want to write it. I'm basically a shy and private person and not confident in my composition skills. I thought someone else must answer the Church Growth Movement, which has created so much division and schism in our midst. Then it hit me. God has prepared me for this task.

May He grant you His spirit of discernment as you read these pages. They will present and test the claims written by both sides of the Church Growth controversy in The Lutheran Church—Missouri Synod. The goal is to reveal which side is pleasing God and which is pleasing people.

Basic to such a testing is this question: is the church a business? Were Jesus, Paul, Martin Luther, and even C. F. W. Walther marketing men, as the Church Growth Movement claims? This ex-marketer-turned-theologian says NO! Marketing is an overarching approach that seeks to please the customer, proclaiming the customer king. True theology can have no customer sovereignty.

The precious Gospel must be sovereign.

Marketing has never helped to grow Christ's true kingdom and never will. His kingdom is not of the business world.

I owe words of appreciation to many—to Jon Vieker for his instigation and consistent encouragement, support, and critique; to Fred Baue for his editorial guidance; to Bob Rothemeyer for his able and timely assistance from Concordia Theological Seminary's library, as well as to Mark and Patti Braden for their assistance; to Paul Raabe for his B.C. wisdom contribution; to my Peacemaker brothers, Frank Pies and Steve Long, who are so dear and close to my soul—may the Lord be with you both always; to Chet and Heloise, my father and mother, who nurtured my body and soul and continue to do so; and to my beloved Bonnie, who is my joy, strength, organizer, and encourager, my helpmate sent by the Lord.

—Dr. Rodney E. Zwonitzer
Dearborn, Michigan
James 4:8a
Palm Sunday, 2002

Introduction

MARKETING
AND CHURCH GROWTH

WHAT IS MARKETING?

Marketing is sometimes thought of as synonymous with selling, peddling one's wares, products, services, or ideas. Though typically sales is a vital function of marketing, it does not define all that the exciting field of marketing entails. In addition, due to the constant stream of advertising that reaches us every day, many equate marketing with commercials and other forms of promotion. But marketing is much more. It is a major factor in contemporary business. Practitioners see marketing as an art, a science, and a discipline within the business world. Some see it within the life of the Christian church as well.

Marketing is about existence, adaptability, and orientation. It is not an end in itself, but provides a very useful tool to make the achievement of an organization's goals a reality. It is a means to the end that all organizations desire—continued existence. At its heart, marketing revolves around keeping organizations, both profit and nonprofit, in existence. Especially in a time of rapid change, organizations must inevitably keep up with trends or they will cease to exist. This is where marketing is at its best—giving an organization the flexibility to not permit a static, once-for-all attitude to predominate, but rather engendering a roll-with-the-punches approach that can prepare for change and even take advantage of it. Effective marketing sets the pace rather than defensively trying to keep pace with changing circumstances.

Marketing is at its best in the most difficult market situations, commonly referred to as "very tough sales." It is most adept at meeting market conditions that are most susceptible to quickly changing variables and where the competition is fierce.

Marketing is about orientation, about a philosophy, about a way of responding to a situation in society and culture. It is orienting (positioning) the organization to its purpose, its objective for existing. Therefore, the term *marketing* speaks of this orientation—it is about "the market." The customer, the one who has needs and desires for products and services—this is one's market. Marketing orientation begins and ends with the focus on the market, the customer, the consumer of products and services. E. Jerome McCarthy's famous university textbook, *Basic Marketing: A Managerial Approach*, defines marketing as "the performance of business activities which direct the flow of goods and services from producer to consumer or user in order to satisfy customers and accomplish the company's objectives." [1]

McCarthy is also famous for speaking of the "Four Ps" of marketing: product, price, promotion, and place. As we say in the trade, this is the "marketing mix." The mix maximizes the blend of what products or services will be offered for sale, at what price, to whom and where they will be sold, and how they will be promoted. This mix of the "Four Ps" is continually being researched, modified, and implemented. The cycle constantly moves with changing customer needs and the responses of competitors. Since marketing is so oriented to the target customer, an organization that does not continue to align itself with customer needs is likely to fail. Thus, marketing seeks to not sell or promote anything that a potential group of customers does not want or need.

PRODUCT OR CUSTOMER?

This runs counter to an older mode that is typically referred to as "product orientation." A classic illustration used in marketing classes is the contrast in the marketing by the Ford Motor Corporation of their highly successful Mustang sports car and their doomed Edsel. The Mustang was born exclusively out of marketing orientation, while the Edsel's design and marketing plan were already conceived prior to any significant market research.[2] Here the focus was not on the customer/market, but rather on the producer and its product. Another example we learned in college was that of a watch. The product-oriented company developed and sold the watch based on what the producer—rather than the customer— thought a watch should do. This approach almost always necessitated the kind of salesmanship that is frequently but incorrectly associated with marketing.

The marketing-oriented watch company went to the potential users of watches and asked them what they desired in a time-keeping device. This made a huge difference in orientation, a new way of doing business. Today, this is described in terms of a paradigm shift. A "paradigm" is that which is used as a model, an example of how things are to be accomplished. Thus, we have seen a paradigm shift in business from the product being the dominant force to the customer being supreme.

For the marketing paradigm shift to be given any chance of succeeding, the entire business must take on this orientation. Thus, beginning with upper management through all levels of the organization, indoctrination and education to this new way of doing business must be implemented.

All resistance to this shift must be overcome and a synergistic commitment to a marketing orientation must be established. The organization continues to measure its performance based on this orientation toward market share. All other objectives and goals stem from and flow out of this overarching objective. Sometimes profit and revenue goals might seem to drive the enterprise, but those who make the numbers work know that what drives these two is the market's response to their product or service offerings. Striving for revenue or profit objectives only happens as customers respond to the marketing plans of the organization. These certainly factor into the development of any marketing plan, but they are derivative, not prescriptive. They are dependent on how well the organization does in marketing—meeting the needs of the target customer base. They are not independent, as even a high-level corporate executive with little or no marketing experience has to learn.

STUDY HARD

Competition is one of the biggest obstacles in meeting customer needs to capture market share. This competition is for a piece of the pie, a percentage of the total market. As with research of the customer's needs, marketing assesses the competition, the controllable variables of the marketplace, and the resources available or securable to the organization. Intense analysis of competitors includes review of their history, their customers, their organizational structure, their products, their pricing, their promotion, and their channels of sales and distribution.

Much effort is expended in gathering data about the competitors in a marketplace. This data is then summarized and analyzed to ascertain the competitor's strengths and weaknesses. Then it is compared to what one's own organization has in each area and to where advantages can be maximized and weaknesses minimized, strengthened, or eliminated. This is like the scouting of opponents in sports or intelligence operations in war. Every bit of data about an opponent is gathered and analyzed to extract even the smallest of advantages to win, in this case, market share.

Much effort is expended on the potential customer, both one who is currently purchasing the product and one who possibly will in the future. Marketers want to know where this customer is, what motivates his purchase decision, who this customer has been purchasing from or plans to purchase from, what his future needs are and what his desires are about this product, and what avenues for promotion he regularly interacts with—magazines, television, radio, newspapers, and, of course, the Internet. Effort will be expended to research what customers and potential customers know about an organization and their reaction to the organization. Also, marketers typically conduct test marketing on real and/or potential customers concerning all elements of marketing mixes, including possible advertising, pricing, products, distribution channels, and so on.

The history of the market is studied intensely as well. Data is gathered and analyzed as to when the market started, its growth rates, its cyclical and seasonal trends, and its various segments. Segmentation analysis of a market based on demographic data has further developed into analysis on two more levels. The first might be called "needs-based segmentation," where the market is categorized according to the customers' interaction with products/services. A second level is called "core-value segmentation." Here the core values of an individual customer become the segment definers that smart leaders keep abreast of to adjust the organization's prime values and role.

To do such research on both the target customer base and the competition, marketing engages in many different types of research techniques. The gathering of statistical data continues to be one of the most important, drawing on many sources, such as the government, private research companies, and industry associations. This is further supplemented by the organization conducting its own research through survey and poll techniques, such as focus groups of customers, where various product features, pricing, and promotional options can be tested for reaction. How a given market breaks down into various segments, for example, by age, gender, geographical location, or income level—these are very important and useful data points for the marketer to learn, monitor, and factor into a marketing plan of attack.

Brand management is becoming very popular in today's marketing world, especially but not limited to consumer products.[3] It studies and manages for organizations such vital topics as the development of a strong and clear brand identity, generation of awareness, commitment to quality, and the fostering of brand loyalty. In essence, it manages three aspects of the organization's brand(s): first, it identifies the brand's promises to the customer; second, it measures "brand equity," or the degree to which the customer perceives that the brand successfully meets these promises; and finally, it monitors and fosters the rational and emotional positive responses that the brand elicits from the customer.[4]

The Eastman Corporation is a prime example of a company that has done a superior job of brand management over the years with its famous Kodak brand. In contemporary markets, General Motors has demonstrated outstanding brand management with its Saturn division.[5]

IMPLEMENTATION

Change is very much a part of current marketing practices—change at a very fast pace. Most companies spend fortunes and deploy key individuals to monitor changing market trends so that adjustments can be made in a timely manner. Marketing constantly seeks to be in a "forward looking" mode. When I first entered the corporate marketing world, I was told that marketing is always looking at least three to five years ahead. Imagine yourself today thinking about how a market will look five or ten years from now. That, in essence, is the larger task of marketing, to be "future oriented."

However, this should not be construed as implying that marketing has no involvement in day-to-day operations. Marketing, like most other disciplines, has its various elements. One way to organize these elements is by time frame (e.g., short-term, mid-term, long-term). Another way to organize is by product (e.g., small autos, luxury autos, trucks, etc., at an auto manufacturer). Brand-management organizational divisions divide management assignments by brands (e.g., the Ford Motor Corporation has Ford, Lincoln-Mercury, Jaguar, Volvo, etc.). The way a large company organizes its marketing elements impacts its overall structure, as organizational charts will likely be built around the marketing focus strategy. Smaller concerns by necessity have a few individuals who handle the full gamut of marketing concerns. For example, in a smaller organization there might be one individual who is essentially responsible for all the marketing activities. The larger the organization, the more specialized the marketing function. For example, there might be separate individuals or departments specifically doing market research, product and/or brand management, advertising, sales, and the like.

When all the necessary information has been collected, it is then organized and developed into a "marketing plan." This constitutes the strategy and tactics—the game plan—for the organization to execute. Every part of the organization is then focused, motivated, and judged based on its support and achievement of the goal. Feedback is constantly collected, analyzed, and formally written into the organization's game plan. Marketing leads the presentation and defense of proposals, which the organization then begins to implement.

Measurement is a very important factor in marketing. The objectives of the marketing plan are constantly measured and monitored as to their levels of successful completion. From this constant monitoring, marketing-mix adjustments can be made expediently to keep up with changing market conditions. What most of us have heard repeatedly from the sports world applies to marketing as well: "Always change a losing game plan." This is a very dynamic, real-time process upon which marketing spends much of its time and effort through leadership and management skills.

MARKETING AND CHURCH GROWTH

Just as marketing provides a valuable tool to organizations that want to be proactive rather than reactive to changing market needs, Church Growth (henceforth CG) claims to provide the same to the Christian church. Some definitions of CG will not mention this, but rather will say that CG wishes to apply sociological and behavioral science to the church. While CG utilizes much from sociological and behavioral science in its research, this is not its major orientation. In its underlying philosophy, CG is very much about marketing. CG is about shifting the church's paradigm from product orientation to market orientation.

CG is about existence, adaptation, and orientation. It claims to be oriented toward the Great Commission (Matthew 28:18–20) of saving lost souls and making them followers of

Christ. This focus is to be the driving motivation and objective that all other activities must support. Without this orientation, the church has no reason to exist or ability to survive.

In our ever-changing world, CG says, the church must have such an orientation to be responsive and viable. CG-style marketing provides such flexibility, with its orientation to mobilize the people of God to be responsive to the culture's needs and desires on the spiritual level. This is initially achieved through research into a congregation's target audience of churched and unchurched people in a given geographical area. CG marketing research will find out what the customer wants. This target audience is asked about the "4 Ps" of the church: product, price, place, and promotion. This research is undergirded by the sociological and behavioral sciences that constantly probe these areas and publish their findings. In addition to developing their own local survey and interview research projects, CG provides professional consultants and a network of pastors and congregations who can assist prospective users of its techniques.

CG is especially concerned about the way the Gospel—the heart and substance of the Christian faith—is packaged, presented, and communicated. In marketing terminology, this translates as the "product." For an eternal saving relationship to begin between a holy God and sinful humans, revelation or communication must occur. Since communication requires a speaker and a listener, CG concentrates on providing a means, a tool to help the church proclaim the Gospel to a culture that in our time has increasingly viewed the previous Gospel packaging and proclamation as irrelevant. CG overcomes this by listening carefully and determining what has caused this rejection by the target hearers, both those currently in churches and those who remain outside any active churched life. Since this is at the heart of the Christian faith (Romans 1:16; 10:14–17), CG concentrates on the substance that must occur in this "speaking-listening" relationship, always focusing on providing communication that will speak the substance of the saving Gospel of Christ and also keep the listener listening.

BE RELEVANT

CG finds that ways of Gospel proclamation and packaging that worked in the past to convert unbelievers and retain them are being rejected by contemporary culture. CG aids in helping churches abandon and/or modify outmoded approaches so that the prospective audience can relate to the Gospel. CG emphatically claims to maintain purity of doctrine in this overhaul of the Gospel's proclamation. Advocates of CG claim to be true to God's Word while repackaging and retooling Gospel outreach. They refer to this maintenance of pure doctrine as "substance."

Previous paradigms or models, which CG refers to as "style," now seemingly alienate a large percentage of people. These paradigms were primarily "product oriented," geared to the language of believers and their spiritual leadership. While the saved can relate significantly and repeatedly to this developed style and vocabulary, the person who is outside the faith group or who has drifted away will now only be reached by a shift in orientation or paradigm. Marketing provides this saving paradigm.

Marketing makes a way for the church to completely research, plan, and then implement a style and language that are oriented for those seeking a closer relationship with God. These target disciples, or "customers," become the driving force behind everything done by churches under this new paradigm: their planning, staffing, and community life. Each and every activity is run through a filter—what does the seeker think and how might he or she react? Everything is now geared to reaching the unchurched and keeping them active.

CG is about rejecting and retiring church paradigms that worked in previous generations but are not effective today. Significant in this paradigm shift to the more modern marketing model is the relationship between the pastor and the congregation. Previously, church models saw significant differences in the responsibilities of the two, with the pastor being the primary communicator of God's Word, the teacher and preacher of the Gospel, while the congregation was seen as the recipient of this orientation, functioning as the support arm for the central clergy function of Word and Sacrament. The congregation provided the officers and chairpersons of the boards and committees supporting the pastoral office, but was not seen as central to reaching the lost with Christ's Gospel. The congregation's role was to support the pastoral office with prayers, finances, talents, and time. The evangelistic outreach of the congregation was limited to inviting the unchurched to worship, Bible study, and other congregational activities, where it was believed that God would make disciples by the power of the Holy Spirit working through the preaching and teaching of the Gospel.

CG views this as inadequate and ineffective in reaching and keeping those who are on the fringes or outside the Christian family. In order to reach them, CG claims, each and every Christian needs to be motivated, equipped, and deployed to make disciples of their contact circles of neighbors, friends, and life acquaintances. A popular way of saying this is "everyone a minister." The clergy's task is to be the enabler, the visionary who brings about this radical transformation of laypeople from passive recipients to frontline disciple-makers. A major factor in this shift is the use of spiritual-gift inventories. These seek to discover what abilities each Christian has been given by God and then employ these abilities for outreach. According to CG, the pastor serves as the motivator, equipper, and cheerleader. This demands a reshaping of the pastor's training as well, with less scholarly theological emphasis and more leadership-skills development. As the pastor becomes the leader of a large group of Christian disciples reaching out with Christ's Gospel to a changing culture, the pastor's ability to manage a significant "marketing plan" must be of the highest quality and effectiveness. CG gears itself to providing this kind of leadership through consultants, seminars, and leadership conferences that give pastors what they have lacked in their traditional seminary training.

WORSHIP AND PREACHING

Since the worship life of a congregation is for most churches the focal point of regular contact, CG devotes much attention to this area. Staying attuned to what visitors and members alike prefer regarding the style of music, the architecture and furnishings of the worship space, and the Gospel proclamation are vital elements to attracting and retaining souls for Christ. CG advocates a variety of worship options for churches. Formal, liturgical worship with hymnals and organs is supplanted by a more relevant, contemporary style featuring guitars, drums, and synthesizers, with the words to songs (not hymns) being displayed overhead. The physical space that suits most guests and regular attendees should not look like churches of the past, with their gothic architecture and pews, pulpits, and stained glass, but rather meld more with modern tastes, employing theater seating with little or no religious symbolism. The traditional preaching of a sermon by a robed authority figure produces a negative reaction from target church members, so the sermon is replaced by a simple talk, which seeks to provide the same theological substance without the listeners even realizing they are being preached to. Much effort is directed at encouraging listeners to not just hear and believe the Gospel message for their salvation, but to be energized to share it with all in their day-to-day living. This is conveyed by hanging signs at church parking lot exits that declare: "You are entering the mission field."

Since contemporary culture has great relevance to the church's Gospel proclamation and all other activities that serve the Great Commission, CG spends ample time and resources constantly monitoring and modifying its "marketing mix" as cultural conditions shift.

CG believes that there is a dangerous disconnect in the church between the mission focus of the church of the apostles and the church culture handed down from the Fathers. CG seeks to emphasize the former. It claims to champion the same ministry banner that Paul wrote about in 1 Corinthians 9:22: "To the weak I became weak, that I might win the weak; I have become all things to all men, that I may by all means save some." Utilizing whatever it can glean from the latest in sociological and behavioral studies as well as marketing, management, and leadership techniques, CG strives to bring the lost to saving faith in Christ. It sees itself as being on safe ground in this orientation, because it believes that similar techniques were utilized not only by Jesus and the apostles, but even by the likes of Martin Luther, C. F. W. Walther, and Francis Pieper. CG does not see itself as a new innovation reflecting secular society; rather, CG restores God-given gifts to faithful stewardship for the growth of His Kingdom. Or so it claims. In the chapters that follow, we will weigh these claims.

1

PEOPLE PLEASERS?
OR BOND-SLAVES TO CHRIST?

CHURCH GROWTH CLAIM:

People no longer feel obligated to be a member of church or go to a church. They will not tolerate irrelevancy. They are not interested in the question, "What does this mean?" Yet, people are very interested in religious issues. They are concerned about "Does it work?" In this time of major paradigm shift, many are suffering from paradigm collision. . . . And many—a growing number—of churches are repackaging the essence of the evangelical, confessional faith, re-tooling the programming of the local church, and re-engineering their attitudes to become missionaries on the mission field.[1]

CONFESSIONAL LUTHERAN CLAIM:

The Lutheran Confessions emphasize what causes true growth. Speaking of the Gospel and the Sacraments, the Augsburg Confession says, "Through these, as through means, He (God) gives the Holy Spirit, who works faith, when and where He pleases, in those who hear the Gospel." (Article V)[2]

CONTROVERSY

Controversy has always been an unfortunate feature of the church militant and always will be until it becomes the church triumphant. It is a myth that there has at times been the God-desired "one united church of Christ" here on earth.[3] Thus, our Lutheran Church—Missouri Synod has been and will continue to be in controversy. Much of our current controversy focuses on the adaptation of the Church Growth Movement to remedy what ails the Synod. Sincere, emphatic, passionate claims have been made for more than 20 years now by those for and those against. Both sides declare the outcome to be critical for the Synod's ultimate survival.

Since all agree that this controversy is truly crucial, pastor and layperson alike need to be well informed of the claims made by both sides. In what follows, I will set forth the issues in basic terms so that the interested layperson will be able to grasp what is at stake. My method will be to set forth the claims of both sides and then cast upon them the light of Scripture and the Lutheran Confessions. First, however, a brief look at introductory questions. Like a journalist, we must ask what, when, why, where, and how this controversy began in the LCMS.

The Church Growth Movement is acknowledged by most to have begun on the mission field in India in the mid-twentieth century. A man named Donald McGavran conducted extensive research into why some churches were growing and others were not. After arriving at what he thought were sound discoveries, he then promulgated his ideas through his teaching at Fuller Theological Seminary in Pasadena, California.[4] He began attracting students from among LCMS pastors and officials in the 1970s. These persons were concerned about the lack of growth in the LCMS. They pointed to membership statistics that showed a decline in the growth rate of congregations, Districts, and the Synod, which resulted in a "plateaued" situation.[5] Almost immediately, opposition arose declaring that the methods of CG are unbiblical and opposed to the Lutheran confession of God's truth. CG opponents contended that the reasons given for the "plateaued" Synod situation were incorrect and that, consequently, the solution was incorrect as well.

Just what is CG? Kent Hunter, a leading advocate, suggests that we use the working definition set forth by the American Society for Church Growth:

> Church growth is that careful discipline which investigates the nature, the function, and the health of Christian churches, as they relate to the effective implementation of the Lord's Great Commission, to make disciples of all peoples (Matthew 28:19–20). It is a spiritual conviction, yet it is practical, combining the eternal principles of God's Word with the practical insights of social and behavioral sciences.[6]

We now examine the claims of both sides of the CG controversy within the LCMS, scrutinizing them in the twofold light of Scripture and the Lutheran Confessions.

CHURCH GROWTH CLAIMS

Many contend that although we have confessed, defended, and practiced pure Christian doctrine more faithfully than many other Christian churches, the LCMS remains "a sleeping giant."[7] While we receive excellent marks on maintaining purity of doctrine, we are severe underachievers on growing Christ's kingdom through outreach and evangelism. We have a triumphal mentality based on our doctrine and our previous growth record, which relied primarily on biological growth (the birth of children of existing members). [8] In other words, we have plateaued. We are in need of major change, new methods of ministry. We are inwardly focused and come up short in packaging and communicating the Good News of salvation by grace through faith in Christ alone. The former paradigm of ministry (Law and Gospel preached in a liturgical Divine Service) is not only ineffective in our modern age of technology and rapid change, but creates barriers to saving lost souls. We need a major overhaul, a rebuilding from the power plant on up if we are to continue to remain on the church landscape. The paradigm, the method, the style needed to bring the "sleeping giant" back to vibrant spiritual life is Church Growth.

OPPOSITION TO CHURCH GROWTH

Critics of CG counter that the preferred solution is incorrect because the diagnosis is incorrect. The plateaued scenario that the Synod finds itself in is a result of the acculturation of Christianity to an individualistic American popular culture. This popular culture dominates most of American society and may come to dominate one of the last bastions of conservative American Christianity, the LCMS. Opponents of CG contend that the style of ministry and the substance of ministry are the same; they cannot be separated. The paradigm of how one does ministry corresponds to the theology confessed, the substance of what one believes.[9] As Kurt Marquart expresses it, "Contrary to popular impression, the differences among the churches are not about trivia, but go to the heart of the Gospel."[10] He shows that the major Christian paradigms—Lutheran, Reformed, and Roman Catholic—constitute the styles of Western Christianity.[11] The approved hermeneutical method for the Lutheran church has always been Law and Gospel arranged around the dual focus of the means of grace (God's Word and Sacraments). This determines the Lutheran way of doing ministry. Importing other methods while still claiming to maintain Lutheran doctrinal substance is not possible. The church must not yield to cultural pressure, but resist and seek to remain "in" the culture but not "of" the culture.

CONFLICTING CLAIMS

St. Paul, in his controversy with the "superapostles" at Corinth, recognized that both he and his opponents claimed apostleship. So it is in the CG controversy. Both sides claim the same precious center: the Gospel. Furthermore, both sides claim the apostolic church for their cause. By necessity, both claim Paul as their champion, since Paul is *the* great missionary and also *the* great theologian. Of course, both sides also claim Jesus as well as Luther and the Lutheran Confessions to support their claims to truth.

Both sides profess to please God in the approach they take to ministry in Christ's stead. Both claim they are contending for the sake of the Gospel and that their opponents are placing stumbling blocks in the paths of their followers. Each side condemns the other as deceivers who do not follow all of God's truth.

PAUL—A THEOLOGICAL CHAMELEON?

One of the most popular Scriptures of the CG Movement is 1 Corinthians 9:22: "I have become all things to all men, that I may by all means save some." This proves beyond any shadow of a doubt, CG claims, that Paul was a CG practitioner. He used any means, any method, any paradigm or style to save a lost soul. And so must we today in the twenty-first century. So should the LCMS.

Many New Testament scholars, however, disagree with this facile interpretation and application.[12] A foundational principle of biblical interpretation is that Scripture interprets Scripture. We do not isolate one scriptural verse from other verses that might help us understand the Word of God. Consider Galatians 1:10: "For am I now seeking the favor of men, or of God? Or am I striving to please men? If I were still trying to please men, I would not be a bondservant of Christ." This verse is critical to the meaning of the whole epistle to the Galatian churches. It is a transition verse from the main thesis (verses 1–9) to the individual thesis to support Paul's argument: "You have deserted the Gospel, which is your salvation."

The Galatians were being deceived by a different gospel, a false gospel that Paul anathematizes. He condemns its preachers to eternal damnation. This is exactly at the heart of the issue in the CG controversy! Paul is either a "people-pleaser" or a "bond-slave to Christ." He cannot be two things at the same time. Nor can we. Either we are pleasing the people or we are bond-slaves to Christ's Gospel.

CG advocates profess that Paul received a marvelous set of "church-growth eyes." This term means "a characteristic of Christians who have achieved an ability to see the possibilities for growth and to apply appropriate strategies to gain maximum results for Christ and his church."[13] The risen Lord Himself supposedly gave Paul these eyes on that momentous day near Damascus. Thus, Paul became a marketing genius who spread Christianity throughout the world. He used any means available, according to this view. He was a true theological chameleon who did whatever it took to save another soul for Christ and grow the kingdom of our Lord. Does the biblical evidence support such claims?

Paul—A Bond-Slave to Christ

Many biblical commentators would dispute the claim that Paul was such a theological chameleon. Although some of the most trusted and sought-out CG experts state that Paul was an any-means-to-the-desired-result kind of pastor, they never provide any substantiated interpretation of the Bible outside of simply making such claims.[14] Close and careful interpretation of the text shows that CG misunderstands Paul. Two prominent scholars conclude: "Paul is not . . . a man pleaser who has diluted the Gospel to achieve a quick and cheap success; he is wholly a servant of Christ."[15]

In Galatians 1, Paul himself refutes the charge of seeking to "please people." His opponents in Galatia accuse him of doing whatever works to win people to Christ. Paul disproves the claim that he is flexible in his doctrine and preaching; he does not teach circumcision when around Jews and noncircumcision when around Gentiles. He is always about the pure Gospel, the Gospel given him personally by direct revelation from Jesus Himself (Galatians 1:11–12). He and the apostles always please God, not people. His call is to be a "bond-slave" to Christ. He offers further evidence of this apostolic calling and defense of the pure Gospel by documenting his trip to Jerusalem, where he established fellowship with James, John, and Peter *only* after it was determined from oral confession that they all believed the same Gospel (Galatians 1:15–2:9).

Ironically, one of the claims being made today is that CG was the style of the apostles. Many LCMS CG speakers refer to a book written by a Methodist theologian that argues the apostolic churches were outreach-oriented.[16] The book deems the following contemporary churches to be "apostolic": Frazier Memorial United Methodist Church, Montgomery, Alabama; New Hope Community Church, Portland, Oregon; Willow Creek Community Church, Barrington, Illinois; Community Church of Joy, Glendale, Arizona; Saddleback Valley Community Church, Orange County, California; The Church on Brady, East Los Angeles, California; New Song Church, West Covina, California; Ginhamsburg United Methodist Church, Tipp City, Ohio; and Vineyard Community Church, Cincinnati, Ohio.

Notice that none of the churches on this list are named "Lutheran." The book identifies only one nominally Lutheran church as apostolic—Community Church of Joy in the Phoenix, Arizona, area. It is affiliated with the Evangelical Lutheran Church in America (ELCA): "This first-generation Lutheran church (LCA) had 'plateaued' and become traditional in near-record time. After a painful transition, [the leaders were persuaded] to 'dream big' and become a mainline denominational church devoted to reaching the unchurched people."[17] This is an example of the drastic change that is being promoted in our midst.

The term "apostolic church" has long been understood to mean the eyewitnesses (apostles) who were guardians of the truth. To be "apostolic" thus means to be about the same as the apostles, as one source puts it: "It is to recognize that the message and the mission of the apostles as mediated through Scripture must be that of the whole church."[18]

Whom do we please and to whom are we enslaved? Paul answers: we please God and are bond-slaves to Christ and His pure Gospel. Since we can only serve one master, we had better assure ourselves that it is God we are pleasing. Jesus said it in these words: "No one can serve two masters; for either he will hate the one and love the other, or he will be devoted to one and despise the other. You cannot serve God and wealth" (Matthew 6:24).

Paul was intent on doing one thing: serving Christ, who had saved him on the cross and called him to preach the Good News. Certainly Paul, like any man, must have wished to be accepted, fulfilled, and successful—but not at the expense of displeasing God. Paul would not dilute, compromise, soften, or minimize the truth given him by Christ just to achieve personal, individual goals. He was bonded to Christ and His Gospel!

Paul's goal was not to please people, but to serve them with the Gospel untainted by human thoughts and ways. In Galatians 1:10 he answers a rhetorical question about persuading people: "Am I trying to please men? If I were still trying to please men, I would not be a servant of Christ."[19] He explains the correct use of persuasion in 2 Corinthians 5:11, where he proclaims the Gospel to influence his audience's conscience. In the first nine verses of this chapter he expresses the desire to be immortal and know that his soul will live forever with God. Therefore, he seeks always "to be pleasing to God." Then, beginning with verse 10, the use of the word *persuade* figures prominently in the text: "For we must all appear before the judgment seat of Christ, so that each one may be recompensed for his deeds in the body, according to what he has done, whether good or bad. Therefore, knowing the fear of the Lord, we persuade men, but we are made manifest to God; and I hope that we are made manifest also in your consciences." He goes on in this chapter to express the content of this persuasion: reconciliation with God through Christ, of which Paul is an ambassador (verse 20). This combines with what he wrote in his first letter to the Corinthians: "for while I was with you, I was determined to know only Jesus Christ and Him crucified." Paul's whole existence from the time of his conversion was to persuade people to be at peace with God (reconciled) through the blood of Christ crucified for the forgiveness of sins. This was his only task: to be a slave and servant of this saving message. What a proclaimer of that message! And what a fierce and valiant defender against all who would dilute or pollute its purity!

A FINAL THOUGHT

Who is carrying on the apostolic church in our day? Who are the people-pleasers and who are the bondservants of

Christ? May the Lord of the church bless our common desire to please Him and to be in bondage to His service in spreading the Gospel and defending it from all attacks.

Hard, pointed questions need to be asked and answered. Do we please Him when we allow individuals—people who have never truly confessed the truth of God or wanted to defend it—to determine the direction of the church? Do we please God when we only desire part of the Word of God to be our norm? These are serious questions that the church of Christ must at all times be cognizant of and answer according to His revealed will.

Another question to ask: does the church need people, or do people need the church? It is quickly apparent that the issue here is one of authority. Who is to be in charge: people or God? Who determines the agenda for the church—the body or the head? CG answers in a coy manner that it is the head, Jesus Christ, but that the body only becomes attached to the head by paying attention to the needs of the unchurched.

The fatal error here is that our needs are determined by the head, Christ, and not by the body, especially not by those who are not yet part of the body or who have become disenfranchised and left the body due to their own choice (see John 6:65–66).

2

THE GOAL OF THE GOSPEL

CHURCH GROWTH CLAIM:

For me the answer depends basically on how one sees the purpose of the Gospel. It is supposed to have an impact that changes the lives of the people who receive it. This is the view of those who make evangelism the controlling purpose of the church.[1]

CONFESSIONAL LUTHERAN CLAIM:

This is the watershed issue: If there really are means of grace, then they are central to the church's life, and then that is the basic meaning and burden of the church's God-given ministry.[2]

OUTREACH OR MEANS OF GRACE

Central to the differing claims in the Church Growth debate is what lies at the core of the life of the church—faith or outreach? The claim of the Church Growth Movement is that outreach is central—that God is primarily concerned about numerical growth. Prominent Lutheran CG advocate David Luecke refers to the "infectious spirit."[3] He argues that

God gives His blessing wherever an infectious attitude of communication occurs, drawing numbers of people who otherwise would not be members of a Christian church. CG claims that an "infectious spirit" was essential at the time of the apostles and remains so today. Luther would condone this notion, CG believes, since this is how God has always grown His church in all ages.

Traditionalists (Confessional Lutherans) reply that CG ignores the Gospel. The church exists only where the Gospel is purely preached and the Holy Sacraments are administered according to the Gospel.[4] This concern for the purity of preaching and the correct usage of the Sacraments is for the sake of the Gospel. There can be no outreach or growth without the pure Gospel. It cannot be stylized, culturalized, modified, or marketed, because its Lord is the same yesterday, now, and forever (Hebrews 13:8). It is not the goal of the Gospel that Christians numerically grow because of their "infectious spirit" or that they do this by circumventing pastors and teachers (see Ephesians 4:11–15), through whom the means of God's grace are given out.

Opponents of CG contend that the true goal of the Gospel—if one can use the term "goal" in conjunction with the Gospel—is that Christ bring an unbeliever into a saving relationship with Himself through His living Word. Notice that in Matthew 7:13–27 Jesus talks about building His house in terms of "those who hear these words of Mine and act on them." He does not specify those who can build a large, numerical following by whatever means, even powerful signs done in His name (verses 21–23). God's Word of forgiveness of sins for Christ's sake by grace through faith is the goal, the heart, and the core of the Gospel.

The question remains: what is the Gospel? Who determines what it is and what it is not? Who determines how the church of Christ will grow by proclaiming this Gospel—in what form, in what style, in what substance?

CG answers that people will be the determiners. They will determine what they like and do not like about any presentation of the Gospel. One of the leading experts of CG, George Barna, makes this point repeatedly in his many books. For example:

> Today, people celebrate their individuality and go to great lengths to be recognized for who and what they are. People avoid group identification in favor of personalized attention. It is considered more blessed to be unique than to be common. Americans no longer care what the Joneses are doing; what they do care about is whether a marketer has adequately understood them to be the unique and important people they believe themselves to be, and that such recognition is reflected through some type of customized or personalized marketing effort.[5]

In fact, CG enthusiastically professes to listen to the individual—the consumer, the customer, the one in the pew—to determine the shape, depth, and content of biblical preaching and teaching. Elsewhere Barna says, "He (Paul) understood that the audience, not the messenger, was sovereign—he was willing to shape his communications according to their needs in order to receive the response he sought."[6]

Confessional Lutherans answer that God's Word is to be the determiner of the Gospel's goal and style of presentation. The Bible contains no admonition to cater to the changing needs of the people. The Word belongs to God and is not to be bent to the desires of its audience. If we turn again to the apostle Paul in Galatians 1, we find that the Gospel he proclaimed was given to him by Christ and not by any human. He proclaimed this Word; he did not try to modify its appeal for a wider audience. This would be impossible for him as a bond-slave to Christ.

SCANDAL

Roland Allen notes a tendency today to avoid preaching the stern doctrine of faith in Christ alone. Christ's claim to be the only Messiah is the "scandal of particularity." Allen says, "We no longer look upon the acceptance of our message as 'deliverance from the wrath to come.' We tend to think that the duty of the church is rather to Christianize the world than to gather out of the world the elect of God into the fellowship of the Son."[7] One of the salient features of Paul's preaching is that it exhibits "no timid fear of giving offence, no suggestion of possible compromise, no attempt to make things really difficult appear easy."[8] Advocates of CG avoid sensitive issues and hard doctrines to keep people engaged with the congregation. Thus, God's Word is limited, so that people won't hear from God what they don't want to hear. There will always be unbelievers and disenfranchised believers among the faithful, so we must not confront them or irritate them to the point of their possibly walking away. Highly touted CG giant Willow Creek Community Church in suburban Chicago, for example, has no cross in its sanctuary. Needless to say, this flies in the face of the biblical mandate.

Confessional Lutherans claim that the motivation for CG is numerical growth at all costs. CG shifts the goal of the Gospel from the justification of sinners to the equipping of believers to win more souls. In this, CG has been seduced by their constant contact with competing theologies, primarily Evangelical.[9]

Certainly all Lutherans, like all Christians, want the church of Christ to grow. Certainly all Lutherans want the church to be relevant to society. The question remains whether this growth is to be about "results" or "means." Dr. Ed Lehman, first President of the Lutheran Church—Canada, understands this issue well:

> Unfortunately, the daily life and activity of the church often causes us to wonder whether theology is really its

heartbeat. The church wants to do those things that will attract people and give it a favorable image in the community. The church struggles for success, acceptance, popularity, relevance . . . but these are results. They are not a starting point. The starting point is the faithful preaching and teaching of the Holy Gospel and the administration of the Sacraments.[10]

Thus Confessionalists point out that there cannot be any real competition between maintaining the pure Gospel and focusing on outreach, since the only way true outreach can occur is via the pure Gospel. Means and ends are integrally linked; any dilution of the pure Gospel will have an impact on the growth of Christ's church and the real goal—salvation of souls. Here again, Galatians 1:6–9 is telling. What we preach and teach as the only true way to salvation must be and must remain dominant in the life of the church. This applies not only to the saved but also to the unsaved.

The CG countercharge is: how then do we attract the unsaved and keep them listening to us so that God might save some? We confess that without the needed faith given by the Holy Spirit working through the means of grace, the unbeliever will be totally unresponsive and hostile to divine revelation. If we try to attract and maintain the interest of unbelievers by playing to their needs and preferences, do we not then exclude God's agenda and His desires for their conversion?

This idea of meeting the felt needs of nonbelievers is a point of contention. Kent Hunter argues that meeting such felt needs serves as a "point of contact" for the Gospel.[11] He places Jesus' ministry of healing in the same category as modern door-openers to the congregation. He suggests that Jesus performed a kind of "bait and switch," using His ministry of healing to lure seekers. But this is false and misleading. While Jesus performed many acts of kindness, they were all focused on His mission as Christ, to suffer and die for sins; those who did not want to go with Him to the cross and be healed of their spiritual disease were not of His family. In the CG movement, one "baits" the unbelievers into being interested in issues peripheral to the Gospel without proclaiming clearly what the faith truly consists of in its entirety. While much "baiting" occurs, few are "switched" to the true purpose of God's church.

The Confessional side is quick to add that CG tends to talk in a confused way about the unchurched, placing in this category without distinction both those who have never believed and those who are in a state of apostasy from saving faith. Undoubtedly, this confusion is unfair to both groups and sidesteps the appropriate scriptural diagnosis and remedy. For instance, would not an unbeliever who has never been exposed to the Lord's Supper have a totally different opinion about "closed Communion" than a former Lutheran? This failure to keep these groups separate is a major flaw of CG. Meeting the felt needs of either group, so Confessionalists say, is unbiblical according to the Lutheran understanding of the church, "which in singlemindedness and enduring faithfulness preserves and propagates the saving truth in the power of the Holy Spirit."[12]

A Final Thought

Drawing heavily upon concepts of pragmatism and marketing, CG supplants the biblical doctrine of justification by grace with a strange admixture of outreach strategies directed (they profess) to nonbelievers while catering to the felt needs of the apostate. Orthodox Lutherans have responded that this approach is foreign to the Scriptures and the Lutheran Confessions. If the center of the church becomes the unchurched, the church itself will be off-center. Instead, we should uphold God's Word and His true center: the means of grace that bring people to faith and sustain the saints eternally.

3

BARRIERS TO THE GOSPEL

CHURCH GROWTH CLAIMS:

The issue is inherited church culture—a means or an end.[1]

We do things right. But then, as I was exposed to Church Growth, I underwent a paradigm shift. I must confess, it was not easy. . . . You see, it isn't enough just to be good at doing things right. You can be doing things very well, but they could be the wrong things.[2]

Our passion is to share this Gospel with a lost and dying world. We will do whatever it takes to be the most effective means of the means of grace. In this regard, we will remove the roadblocks to growth. We will take away anything that hinders the easy flow of the means of grace.[3]

CONFESSIONAL LUTHERAN CLAIMS:

Ashamed of the Liturgy? Ashamed of the Sacrament? Ashamed of Jesus? No, good mission work is not done with half-way measures, while hiding our holiest jewels under a bushel![4]

Certain thought-patterns in American culture, however appropriate in the earthly kingdom, can raise problems when brought into the spiritual kingdom of the church. The American philosophy of pragmatism aims only at quantifiable results, assuming that the desired outcomes can be produced when the barriers are removed. Such a view—concerned only with the question "Does it work?"—often neglects issues of objective truth and the radical consequences of the Fall.[5]

TIMES HAVE CHANGED

A barrier is commonly understood to be an obstruction, such as a fence or wall, that hinders or restrains. Typically barriers keep out the undesirable, protecting and marking off something precious from that which would infiltrate to damage or destroy. Church Growth advocates in the LCMS claim that Lutherans in this country have erected "barriers" that do not protect and preserve the pure Gospel, but instead restrict this saving Gospel from being efficacious. They view these barriers as "stylistic," that is, not having to do with the main tenets of the faith, instead reflecting an inherited Lutheran cultural way of believing, teaching, and confessing. As Kent Hunter contends: "This is the key question: Is the Word being faithfully preached and are the Sacraments being rightfully administered when we are using unproductive packaging and irrelevant styles?"[6] Let's make a list of these "barriers" proposed by CG spokesmen: liturgy, vestments, hymnals, organs, traditional church architecture and furnishings, sermons, and doctrines such as closed Communion and ordination limited to men.

What has happened to make these barriers be seen today as restrictive instead of protective? Change seems to be the answer. Fast-paced change in culture and society in the last forty years—the result of individualism, technology, relativism, and consumerism—has made many traditions obsolete.

CG enthusiasts believe they can meet the challenge of change with effective outreach and doctrinal soundness.[7] But what they define as "effective" is up for debate; they equate it with "courageous." "Courageous" means pastors and congregations who rebel against their inherited Lutheran culture and make radical changes to attract and retain a growing membership.[8] CG says, "The very fact that Scripture reports numbers (and such large ones) ought to convince even the simplest that God wants more. His clearest yearnings are maximal: all."[9]

What has been singled out as the biggest barrier for churches of the Lutheran confession has been the Lutheran way of worship, which is found to be a culturally conditioned tenet of the German Lutheran church and therefore not part of inherited Christian teachings and practices. David Luecke relates the story of how one Lutheran music director discovered this barrier:

> A classically trained organist and choir director, he knew intimately the rich Lutheran musical heritage. But he found a new orientation when he accepted Pastor Oesch's invitation to visit some of the large Evangelical churches in the area to see what he could learn. He was impressed by the vibrancy of the music and singing along with the effectiveness of outreach to large numbers. This led him to the pivotal question, is there anything I am doing musically that is a barrier to effective outreach?[10]

Thus, the music of the historic Lutheran church is seen as a barrier. Music becomes a "style" issue, in which varying musical formats must be permitted to coexist alongside traditional Lutheran worship approaches. Further, CG believes that marginal church attendees and those who are seeking out a spiritual home for the first time need music and worship planned and implemented according to the guiding principle found in Acts 15:19: "We should not make it difficult for the Gentiles who are turning to God."[11]

The Confessionalists respond that this is extremely dangerous. Why should individuals who do not yet know or believe in God's plan of salvation or who have rejected it be asked what they want and don't want in worship? To take the holy, precious thoughts of God and let them be altered by undiscerning unbelievers—or, even worse, by those who once believed but have fallen away because of God's words (see John 6:61–66)—is totally foreign to the history of Christ's church. Scripture is replete with warnings not to give in to such pressures (for example, see Jeremiah 15:19–21; Isaiah 6:9–13; and 2 Timothy 4:1–5).

Even more devastating is CG's program to "adjust the worship mix" to achieve whatever results are targeted. This ignores what God promises to give through His Word and Sacraments. The CG approach embodies "theological aimlessness," with no understanding of the means of grace and their Gospel power.[12] A congregation that refrains from frequent celebration of the Lord's Supper so as not to offend or annoy visitors is ashamed of the precious Gospel delivered in the Holy Supper. Did not the Lord speak about those who were ashamed to confess Him before an adulterous generation (see Mark 8:38)? We believe in a proud, loving proclamation of the feast of victory even in the presence of the unbelieving who may come among us. This is a witness to our belief in the promises of God found in this sacrament and our reliance upon His means of grace in giving, sustaining, and growing our faith.

WORSHIP AS ADIAPHORA?

Diversity and freedom in worship are claimed as confessional principles by CG, citing particularly the Adiaphoristic Controversy of the sixteenth century.[13] Worship is lumped under the heading of "adiaphora"—that which is neither commanded nor forbidden by Scripture. This is then coupled with CG's *sedes doctrinae* ("seat of doctrine," that is, a particular text of Scripture used as the primary foundation of a doctrine), 1 Corinthians 9:19–23, which "proves" that the church should become all things to all people so as to save some. Worship is thus changed for the sake of those not attached to any church at all and for the weak in faith, those "baptized, unchurched, nominal Christians."[14]

Supporters of traditional Lutheran worship practices argue that the 1 Corinthians text is being misinterpreted. Gregory Lockwood expresses this position well in his commentary on this passage:

> For the sake of church growth, some advocates have taken 1 Corinthians 9:19–23 as a pretext for scrapping traditional liturgy and hymnody and abandoning biblical but potentially offensive themes of Christian preaching (sin and grace, Law and Gospel, the centrality of Christ crucified). This passage, so they claim, permits whatever changes a pastor or church may deem necessary to appeal to unbelievers. However, 9:19–23 is about preachers accommodating themselves, not the message. It's not about giving up the truth of the Gospel, or compromising it, or leaving it unspoken, or assuming that people naturally know it—they don't![15]

Lockwood articulates the Confessional Lutheran position regarding this passage, that Paul is not condoning carte blanche accommodation to cultural pressures to change what is offensive to the unchurched. Rather, Paul says we should be conversant with the culture and use this knowledge "in the service of bringing salvation to the lost."[16] Examples from Paul's ministry provide the church with clear applications of the principle of "doing whatever it takes to save some" (9:22b). We can see these in Acts 13:16–41; 17:22–31; 21:37–22:2; 1 Corinthians 1:18–25; 2:2; 10:32; and Galatians 1:6–9.[17]

Does the Gospel Need "Repackaging"?

Advocates of CG are concerned with how one "tools the programming of the local church."[18] This presumes that since cultures are constantly changing, then the presentation of the Gospel must also shift. The current shift in our cultural setting is to a "mission orientation."[19] Such orientation takes place when the "repackaging" of the church occurs. Drawing on diagnostic methods and terminology from the managerial and sociological disciplines, this means assessing the likes and dislikes of target audiences of uninvolved community members. Then programs and services are provided that cater to these preferences. This supposedly allows God's means of grace to "change the church" into taking the Great Commission seriously.[20] Such change in packaging is explained as "the simple truths carried in various changing forms."[21] The barriers that CG targets for removal include pews, sermons, closed Communion, male-only clergy, and the liturgy and hymns: "The desire is to strip away anything that gets in the way of people hearing the Gospel, whether they are unchurched people hearing it for the first time, or Christians who need to grow in the grace and knowledge of our Lord and Savior Jesus Christ."[22]

Confessionalists respond that the church's life "cuts across all cultures."[23] Christ calls sinners out of the world to be His people. The Gospel calls sinners out of the world's culture to His kingdom, the church. Christ would have the secular culture conform to His church. Indeed, by the year 400 A.D., the church had conformed the Roman Empire to the principles of Christ. The kingdom of grace is called, led, and sustained by His Word, not by any human needs or wants or desires or traditions. This Word alone is to be the determiner of Christian culture as developed in the church. The church has historic roots, catholic and apostolic. This means that its traditions of worship transcend cultures. They have existed for centuries, not as the worship of individuals or congregations, but rather as what Christians over time have accepted as the norm for worship. The Lutheran Confessions themselves speak highly of the benefits and blessings of such maintenance of historic orders and rites of worship:

> Furthermore, we gladly keep the ancient traditions set up in the church because they are useful and promote tranquility, and we interpret them in the best possible way, by excluding the opinion that they justify. But our enemies falsely charge that we abolish good ordinances and church discipline. We can claim that the public liturgy in the church is more dignified among us than among the opponents. If anyone would look at it in the right way, we keep the ancient canons better than the opponents. (Apol. XV, 38–39).[24]

Orthodox Lutherans resolve that in a cultural climate of diversity and pluralism, we need to recover the transcendence and universality of the church culture. This transcendence is violated when biblical principles are abandoned for the sake of popular culture. Kurt Marquart argues:

> What we need more than ever before is a truly compelling vision of the importance of "church," and that cannot be created from opinion surveys among outsiders. It must arise from the deepest nature of Christian faith itself. Only a church which doesn't give a rap about what Hollywood or "Baby Boomers" or the Supreme Court think, can be taken seriously by anyone with any respect for religion—never mind Christianity![25]

In reality, according to the Lutheran Confessions, adiaphora is not the inherited rites and hymns, but rather ceremonies such as the use of salt and oil in infant Baptism, the laying on of hands at confirmation, the ringing of bells, and the like.[26] Matthew Harrison asks and answers two vital questions:

> May Article X of the Formula of Concord be used to justify individual pastors' or congregations' claims to

absolute liturgical freedom in modern America? Is Article X intended to keep larger church bodies from setting specific liturgical standards, and requiring pastors and congregations to adhere to these standards for the sake of order, decorum, edification and love? Absolutely no, to both questions. The nature of liturgical consensus must continue to be discussed among American Lutherans. Let no one assert that a desired liturgical unity and uniformity is *eo ipso* "unlutheran." For then Chemnitz, Andreae, Selnecker, and the Lutheran Confessions are "unlutheran." Ceremonies are "free," but "this liberty is not license." [27]

The Confessions state clearly that in times of "confessional attack and suppression," the church must consider all things as vital to defending the pure Gospel. Confessionalists argue that the influx of CG theory from outside Lutheranism has brought about this very situation in which the pure Gospel is under attack. Thus, in such a time of crisis, no truly Lutheran ceremony or tradition that is based on God's Word should be considered adiaphora or a matter of indifference. The Lutheran Confessions teach this:

> We also believe, teach, and confess that in a time when confession is necessary, as when the enemies of God's Word want to suppress the pure teaching of the holy gospel, the entire community of God, indeed, every Christian, especially servants of the Word as the leaders of the community of God, are obligated according to God's Word to confess true teaching and everything that pertains to the whole of religion freely and publicly. They are to do so not only with words but also in actions and deeds. In such a time they shall not yield to the opponents even in indifferent matters, nor shall they permit the imposition of such adiaphora by opponents who use violence or chicanery in such a way that undermines true worship of God or that introduces or confirms idolatry. [28]

Furthermore, Lutherans believe that one should be careful about what is labeled "adiaphora." We may not use "adiaphora" as an excuse to make our practice of the faith look like that of a confession that is contrary to ours (see S D X.5). CG has adopted worship and preaching styles that are contrary to our Lutheran confession of the pure Gospel.[29] Marquart points out that "belief systems are not like strings of pearls, where adding or taking some pearls away still leaves the rest unchanged. Theologies, whether true or false, are more like living organisms, in which every part influences, and is influenced by, every other."[30] Blending bits of Baptist or Pentecostal worship with Lutheran worship doesn't take the best from these other confessions—it injects their false theology. Pure doctrine leads to pure worship; false doctrine leads to false worship. False worship leads to false doctrine; pure worship leads to pure doctrine. *Lex orandi, lex credendi; lex credendi, lex orandi.* The Lutheran Church has a distinct confessional identity. It has specific ways of confessing the truth—truth handed down through the ages of the church, truth that is to be proclaimed in its purity, truth that finds its most fitting expression not only in the pulpit but at the altar.

To permit diversity or change for the sake of a more "generic Christianity" is contrary to what a Lutheran Christian has always believed, confessed, and practiced.[31] Note what the writers of the Book of Concord stated in their preface:

> To repeat once again for the last time, we are minded not to manufacture anything new through this work of concord nor to depart in either substance or expression to the smallest degree from the divine truth, acknowledged and professed at one time by our blessed predecessors and us, as based upon the prophetic and apostolic Scripture and comprehended in the three Creeds, in the Augsburg Confession presented in 1530 to Emperor Charles V of kindest memory, in the Apology that followed it,

and in the Smalcald Articles and the Large and Small Catechisms of that highly enlightened man, Dr. Luther.

They go on to add what the Confessionalist side claims for itself in the CG controversy:

> On the contrary, by the grace of the Holy Spirit we intend to persist and remain unanimously in this truth and to regulate all religious controversies and their explanations according to it. (Preface to the Book of Concord, 23)

When the centrality of the Divine Service focuses not on the means of grace but rather on emotional appeals and moralistic teachings, there is great danger that the people will take over the service. Sainted LCMS President Dr. A. L. Barry stated the obvious: "It seems just a tad inappropriate to permit those who know the very least about the Christian faith and about our Lutheran confession to determine the forms by which this faith and this confession are expressed in public worship."[32]

A FINAL THOUGHT

The term "barrier" here is not a negative. It reflects the scriptural understanding that those not of the faith cannot possibly believe or worship without the means of grace intervening and creating faith. Paul devotes a whole chapter to this issue in 1 Corinthians 2. Those who have been raised in a Fundamentalist or Reformed church will find it difficult to relate to incarnational, sacramental theology. Alluding to the Reformation beginnings of these movements, one could state succinctly, "What has Wittenberg to do with Geneva?" Frustrated Baptists who are looking for a new church home will likely not be excited to experience Lutheran liturgy and Law-Gospel preaching for the first time.

The old adage states: "Where there's smoke, there's fire." In the CG controversy, smoke is being raised—issues of liturgy, hymnody, what to call the sermon, and so on—but all are the result of the fire, what is being done with the Holy Gospel. When one puts the doctrine of justification (and its expression in traditional worship) in a subservient position to a missionary zealousness that seeks to gain relevancy by constantly shifting means, then vigilant maintenance of the pure Gospel gives way to techniques and programs that people can control and measure. Kent Hunter says, "Of course, we want doctrinal purity, and we desire to be confessionally strong. But our primary task is not to defend the truth, but to share it. That is the real war and the essential battle that is before us." [33]

The means of grace are certainly barriers to unbelievers. That's one reason why we practice closed Communion. How the precious means of grace could in any way be barriers to believers is beyond comprehension. Humans in their natural state cannot value the means of grace as they should be valued, as the precious jewels of the faith. In Christ's parable, the Gospel is the "pearl of great price." Those who reject the means of grace as the heart and soul of the church's inreach and outreach are not Lutheran, not true to the Holy Scriptures. This we Lutherans believe, confess, and, with God's blessings, can practice together in unity and harmony.

4

THIRD BASE MINISTRY?
OR RUNNING THE BASES?

CHURCH GROWTH CLAIMS:

The word "sermon" is falling into disuse. It simply doesn't mean much to people anymore. That is why many Church Growth paradigm pastors identify what many of us previously called "the sermon" in the bulletin as "the message." This is an interesting example of a change of nonessentials. There will be some, primarily traditionalists, who will be appalled that people don't even know what to call a "sermon" anymore. There will be other traditionalists who will conclude that when I preach it sounds like a speech or a talk—even though the orthodox content (sin and grace, Law and Gospel, means of grace) are all there.[1]

The tradition of Lutheran worship leaders is to be proclaimers rather than communicators. The tradition puts distance between them and the congregation as audience.[2]

CONFESSIONAL LUTHERAN CLAIMS:

Typical Lutheran preaching, we are told, fails to establish this contact because this preaching does not deliver what the person in the pew wants to hear. Thus, it does not "communicate," and must be changed. . . . What Lutheran preaching needs to deliver is not "communication" but rather "proclamation."[3]

Certainly, the Scriptures give guidance for life, and the Third Use of the Law has an important function in the Christian life. But pastors must be very careful to avoid the cultural temptation to preach sermons that are merely "therapeutic," as opposed to bringing their listeners to repentance, through the Law, and to faith, through the Gospel of free forgiveness through the death and resurrection of Jesus Christ.[4]

I am extremely concerned that the quality and content of our pastors' sermons are not just acceptable, not just good, not even very good, but excellent, truly excellent. Our pastors' sermons should reflect their high and holy calling in the Lord that our pastors have to shepherd the flock of God over whom they have been made overseers by the Holy Spirit (Acts 20:28). The people do not attend church to hear the pastor amuse them, or give them a pep talk, or a psychotherapy session in feeling better about themselves. The people of God come to hear a word from God through the pastor's sermon.[5]

AN APT ANALOGY

Preaching does not command the attention it should in the Church Growth debate. CG seems to want to avoid the issue. When advocates of CG engage the subject, they criticize traditional Lutheran preaching as needing a major overhaul. Confessionalists respond that this is unbiblical, unlutheran, and hazardous to the Gospel. Admittedly, it is frustrating to talk about preaching without analyzing sermons in their entirety. We will have to focus on generalities. But we will also look at an excellent little sermon preached by Rev. Don Matzat.[6] It is so pertinent to this discussion that it provides the chapter title.

On a recent Issues, Etc. interview, we discussed the subject of sanctification. My guest, a Reformed theologian, compared the various views on sanctification with a wind-up doll. When you wind-up the Pentecostal doll, it speaks in tongues. The Reformed doll grabs the third use of the Law. The Holiness doll goes after perfect sanctification. And what about the Lutheran doll? Well, from [the Reformed theologian's] perspective, when you wind up the Lutheran doll, it simply goes in circles.

After giving some thought to what he said, I came to the conclusion that he was right. Lutherans do go in circles. Or, to put it into baseball parlance, we hit for the cycle.

Let me explain ... Think of a baseball diamond. At home plate, put the Law. At first base, the Gospel. At second base, faith. At third base, good works or the Christian life.

Now then, when an unbeliever steps up to the plate, the first thing he is hit with is the Law. He becomes aware of his sin before God. This drives him to first base, where the Gospel confronts him with the Good News of the forgiveness of sins, life, and salvation.

As he rounds first base, the Holy Spirit produces faith, causing him to grasp the Good News and rejoice in his salvation. As he rounds second base, faith, being no idle notion, brings the Holy Spirit and produces good works. His life is changed as he motors to the good works of third base.

In the third-base coaching box there are a variety of coaches holding up the "stop" sign. "Stop," they cry. "Come over here and speak in tongues to get really holy." Others offer the dream of perfect sanctification. Some promote their own evangelical house rules—don't drink, smoke, dance, or go to movies. Some theologians of the Reformation group are debating the third use of the Law.

The apostle Paul is also in the coach's box, waving the runner through. "Get to home plate," he shouts. "Keep going! Don't stop at third base." So the runner rounds third and heads for home, saying to himself, "Wow! I am really a good, holy Christian."

As he gets to home plate, he is in for a surprise. He gets nailed by the Law again. This time, though, it is not Romans 1 and 2, but rather Romans 7. "So, you think you are really hot stuff," the Law says to him. "Quite a good Christian, eh? You are merely a wretched man born out of the wretched root of your father, Adam."

Filled with sorrow and contrition, he wanders back up the first base line declaring, "Almighty God, merciful Father, I am a poor, miserable sinner . . ." This time as he gets to first base, he not only hears the Good News of forgiveness, but his pastor is waiting for him with words of absolution—"I forgive you!" He also hears Jesus saying to him, "Take and eat, this is My body and blood given for your forgiveness."

"This is fantastic," he cries as his faith is again built up and his heart is filled with great joy. He heads toward second base renewed in his faith. As a result, his behavior, actions, and attitudes are again being adjusted. This time, as he arrives at third base, the coach's box is filled to overflowing. Everyone wants him to stop. One former football coach offers "Promise Keeping." Someone else wants to put a "What would Jesus do?" bracelet on his wrist. Bearded psychologists are there offering self-esteem, support groups, and help for his wounded inner child.

The apostle Paul is still there waving him home. But this time he is being backed up with some of the saints of the past—Martin Luther and C. F. W. Walther. So our faithful base runner heads back to home plate only to get clobbered with the Law again.

He continues to run the bases and his understanding of sin deepens. He grows in the knowledge of the grace of God in Christ Jesus. His faith increases and good works freely flow from his life. Much to his amazement, as he reads the Bible, he discovers that this is exactly what God wants for him.

As he grows, he learns to love the worship of the church. He discovers that various elements of the liturgy deal with either the Law, Gospel, faith, or good works. The traditional hymnody of the church enhances his experience of Christian growth. He sings with enthusiasm "Alas, My God, My Sins Are Great," "Jesus, Thy Blood and Righteousness," "My Faith Looks Up to Thee," and "May We Thy Precepts, Lord, Fulfill." In so doing, he is running the bases again and growing.

So, we go in circles! Fight the good fight, and run the good race, but whatever you do—don't stop at third base!

This sermon illustrates differences over preaching. CG advocates "third base ministry," while the Lutheran Confessionalists promote "running all the bases." Third base ministries tend to focus on sanctification issues—now that you're saved, this is the way to live your life in Christ. Sermons will be topical; that is, they do not follow the lectionary of the Church Year. In one CG congregation, the pastor polls the congregation to find out what topics they would like to hear about. The pastor then schedules these topics for the year—sex, taxes, money management, parenting, and so on. His "messages" consist of lists of what to do and to not do, along with guidelines for improvement and correction. The various doctrines of the faith are not requested by the people, nor are they selected by CG preachers.

They have moved to this type of preaching under the influence of Evangelical churches. They can see the attention and enthusiasm the people in the pews have for such sermons;

David Luecke calls these sermons "audience-centered."[7] This is fueled by the application of marketing principles. By doing demographics and/or segmentation analysis, a target audience is identified that the church would like to reach. This targeted group is then surveyed to find out what concepts or practices of the church are "turn offs" or "turn ons." All hindrances to the desired response from the audience are removed—that is, the preacher's traditional clothing, the pulpit, the specialized language of the Bible and Christian church, even the term "sermon."[8] Especially catered to are those who were one-time active church members, but were driven away by the attitudes and practices of the church.[9] We are now in the era of religious consumerism: the audience is supreme; the customer comes first.[10]

Confessionalists respond that preachers are called and ordained servants of the Word. Their agenda is driven by the One they are speaking for, not the ones they are speaking to. They serve the Word, both the Word Incarnate and the inspired Word of God that carries in its essence the promise and fulfillment of man's salvation. Why should those to whom God desires to speak set the agenda? They are the ones who need God's Word. The doctor, not the patient, is supposed to write the prescription.

The Scriptures are replete with evidence for the Confessionalist position. Consider John 6:52–69. Here Jesus responds to the Jews who are arguing among themselves about His claim to give His flesh to eat: "Truly, truly, I say to you, unless you eat the flesh of the Son of Man and drink His blood, you have no life in yourselves" (verse 53). Verse 59 notes that He speaks this in the synagogue; He is preaching. Some who follow Him do not like this heavy doctrinal teaching and therefore stop following Him (verse 66). The Confessionalists point out that if Jesus had been a CG practitioner, He certainly would have urged these former followers to forgive Him and return to remain part of His flock. However, Jesus shows no such tendency to change His message to accommodate those who might fall away. Instead, He turns to the remaining disciples and challenges them: "You do not want to go away also, do you?" (verse 67).

CG focuses on communication. If by "communication" CG means such things as enunciation, pronunciation, voice usage, public-speaking techniques, and the like, then Confessionalists agree that these are necessary. But for CG advocates, the heart of the emphasis on communication is audience response. Anything that distances the preacher from the audience distorts or negates meaningful communication. Paul is cited here as the biblical model—especially, as Luecke reports, in his tendency to be "personal."

Furthermore, Luecke is greatly concerned about the supposed trend among Confessional Lutherans to downplay preaching in favor of the Lord's Supper. This, he charges, is "sacramentalism."[11] He contends that Lutherans have always favored the preached Word over the Sacraments.[12] Kent Hunter says that the real work of the preacher is to equip the people to do ministry, not merely to preach the Gospel and administer the Sacraments. He calls traditional Word and Sacrament ministry "a major corruption of the Lord's strategy which God intended for the explosive expansion of His kingdom."[13] The pastor is to function as the inspirer, the motivator, the equipper of the congregational members so that they may communicate the Gospel to the world.

Confessionalists speak of the necessity to remain Law-Gospel preachers, following Walther's teaching on how to "rightly distinguish from each other the Law and the Gospel."[14] This is to proclaim the Law so clearly that "every mouth may be closed, and all the world may become accountable to God" (Romans 3:19).

Although the relationship between the Office of the Public Ministry and the priesthood of all believers is the subject of a later chapter, we must briefly note here that this relates to the confusion over the purpose of the Gospel. If one views evangelism as more important than the doctrine of justification, then preaching will necessarily focus on what the unchurched want to hear. And the unchurched say, "We will have no man preaching to us! Give us drama, skits, self-help lists, moral persuasion, but no preaching!" Articles of doctrine are to be avoided. The frequency of the Lord's Supper is diminished since one does not want to alienate potential worshippers. As one Confessionalist observes: "True Law and Gospel preaching is becoming more of a rarity in our day. Instead of Law preaching we hear 'whiny exhortations' and . . . moralizing and tirading against the evils of the day."[15]

Robert Schaibley clarifies the difference between communication and proclamation. He argues that communication is synergistic: "Communication requires the cooperation of the hearer; without that cooperation there is no communication."[16] In contrast, proclamation is monergistic: "Proclamation requires the presence (obviously), but not necessarily the cooperation of the hearer; even without that cooperation proclamation occurs (assuming the Gospel has been voiced)."[17]

Schaibley advances a threefold role for Lutheran preaching as proclamation: "(a) to bring the Biblical Gospel to the people; (b) to bring the people into the one historic church; and (c) to confront error which threatens the people of God."[18] But this causes a major point of disagreement between CG advocates and Confessionalists:

> All this sounds fine, and we think that it is meet, right, and proper. However, the culture, the world, and our own sinful flesh unite to demand something else out of the sermon. A sermon to many is a behavioristic message. It is a spiritual locker room address, in which a spir-

itual coach gets a spiritual team ready to "go out there and win one for Jesus!" Moreover, a sermon to many is downright moralistic, laying down the "dos" and "don'ts."[19]

This takes us back to the basic issue: is the sermon about catering to the people's opinions or is it about serving God's demands? For the sake of debate, let's put the very best construction on the CG resolve to satisfy the "unchurched" expectations for a message. This requires "bait-and-switch" preaching: "bait" them with introductions, stories, illustrations, and narratives that will catch and hold their attention, and then sneak in the Gospel, "switching" their train of thought to the cross of Christ.

Confessionalists oppose CG because it sacrifices the pure Gospel at the altar of evangelism—not real evangelism, though, but an attempt to sell the unchurched whatever generic gospel they might be inclined to buy, as established by marketing polls. For example, CG approves of Promise Keepers (PK) without any doctrinal reservations.[20] PK leader Bill McCartney vigorously promotes the breaking down of all barriers, including denominational. He believes that important biblical doctrinal teachings on the Sacraments and fellowship are divisive, irrelevant, and sinful. He urges men to "cut each other some slack" on such contended biblical doctrine.

Lutherans must answer: even if PK doesn't care about all of Jesus' words, Lutherans do! PK doesn't care about the means of grace, His Word and Sacraments. In fact, PK says these are divisive. So let's stop talking about them and cut each other some slack. PK doesn't care if men get placed back under the Law. PK doesn't care about confusing Law and Gospel. But Lutherans do! Isn't it amazing, Confessionalists ask, that Lutheran CG advocates can declare no disagreement with PK's confession, when PK openly contradicts what Lutherans confess? One of their seven promises is: "Reach beyond any racial and denominational barriers to demonstrate the power of Biblical unity."[21] This flies in the face of what Lutherans have always believed vital in preaching: to proclaim all truth and expose all errors that would lead the sheep astray. If Lutheran pastors say they find no theological problems with PK, it is likely that their preaching betrays this same lack of discernment.

CG typically cites a "statistic" that the average attention span today is only twelve minutes, but Schaibley points out the ridiculousness of the so-called "attention span" problem. Everyone's attention span is naturally broken many times in normal listening; thus, the pastor will inevitably lose everyone's attention at points in his sermon. But this does not mean that sermons should be shorter. Schaibley advises to "work toward clear Law, clear Gospel, and fret not about the average attention span." He also disagrees with the notion that one must decode the text into twenty-first century language. He responds by saying that this is an allegorical approach to preaching, placing the text in a new context. "But if not that, if not allegory, what ought we to do? We need to translate the twentieth-century mind-set into the first century or the Old Testament text."[22]

A FINAL THOUGHT

Lutherans have always valued the "sermon" as a most important part of the Divine Service. As Luther said: "You know that the greatest divine service is the preaching of the Word of God, and not only the greatest divine service [worship] but also the best we can have in every situation."[23]

The charges of both sides about the current state of preaching are serious, with the very Gospel itself at stake. One side claims that the other is diluting the pure Gospel to increase membership, while the other side claims that opponents are erecting barriers so the Gospel cannot succeed.

A pastor tells the story of hearing his father (also a pastor) continually proclaim that we Lutherans preach the pure Gospel. So one day the son inquired of his father, "What is this pure Gospel?" To which the father responded: "I don't know, but we have it."

That is my assessment of too much of the preaching in our midst: we have the pure Gospel, but we don't seem to be overly concerned about it; we just take for granted that we have it. Too many skate over the important matter of making sure there is no confusion of Law and Gospel. Don't preach all the counsel of God's Word, for the people in the auditorium seats or pews won't tolerate it. Just intently concentrate on presenting fresh, captivating messages that don't sound like sermons. Fake them out so that when they think they're not hearing God's Word, they are!

What Paul warned the young preacher Timothy about is now upon us:

> In the presence of God and of Christ Jesus, who will judge the living and the dead, and in view of His appearing and His kingdom, I give you this charge: Preach the word; be prepared in season and out of season; correct, rebuke, and encourage—with great patience and careful instruction. For the time will come when men will not put up with sound doctrine. Instead, to suit their own desires, they will gather around them a great number of teachers to say what their itching ears want to hear.

Because of entertainment evangelism, Lutheran Law and Gospel proclamation has been derailed, replaced, repackaged, and retooled with Evangelical, Pentecostal, Pietistic, and Revivalist preaching emphases and techniques.

God's promise to build and sustain His church on the solid rock of the pure Gospel is no longer trusted. Instead, trust is given to other things: marketing, sociology, management techniques. The church, which for generations has been built by grace through faith in the pure Gospel and Sacraments, must return to its God-given "catholic" heritage of preaching. Two great preachers in this heritage make the same admonition: "A student of theology ought to make proper preaching his highest aim. For if he is unable to preach, he does not belong in the ministry. . . . The worth of a true minister of the church lies exclusively in his ability to preach properly. . . . Preaching is the central element of every divine service" (C. F. W. Walther). "Therefore, when God's Word is not preached, one had better neither sing nor read, or even come together" (Martin Luther). [24]

5

EFFECTIVE OR FAITHFUL?

CHURCH GROWTH CLAIMS:

I don't like the word "success." I don't personally use it anymore. "Success" in our society means things like material gain, and the spotlight is on me (if I'm successful) and so forth, and those aren't the proper kind of motives for church growth. Really what church growth is more concerned about is being effective.[1]

In times of social change, the path to faithfulness in ministry is to discern and follow the Spirit's lead toward changes in style of communicating and organizing that offer promise for greater effectiveness in the unchanging mission of churches with Lutheran substance.[2]

Total Quality Management is a process for achieving high quality within an organization. It has its basis in the understanding that quality is measured by the customer and that quality means meeting or exceeding the customer's expectations 100 percent of the time. With this understanding of quality, the Total Quality Management process employs organizational principles and resources in ways to meet this quality goal. . . . This book develops the translation of those processes into the Christian church. . . . Yet we may not have ever associated the term customer with the church. Because quality is always centered on the customer's expectations, it is essential also that congregations understand this term.[3]

CONFESSIONAL LUTHERAN CLAIMS:

Therefore, it is spiritually harmful when anything other than faithfulness by pastor or people to the pure Gospel and Sacraments of Christ is used to measure the "health" of a congregation. (1 Corinthians 2:2)[4]

The gospel does not become powerful when and if something is added. It is powerful because Jesus is both its content and its administrator. Every false teaching can be evaluated and described in terms of what that false teaching tries to add to the gospel to make it work.[5]

We need to cultivate a theological dislike for the word "accountability." . . . Moderns have come to believe that every problem has a "managed solution." . . . A good manager gets results! Seek ye first technique and principles, and all results will follow you. Unruly problems only need the right rule. In one instance, the growth experts told congregations, serving a class of people who have, for at least a century, been cold to church membership, that the "traditional church" was the problem.[6]

THE GREAT COMMISSION

Both sides in the Church Growth controversy recognize from the Synod's statistics that there is an evident plateau in membership. What is disputed is the diagnosis of the cause of the problem and its remedy. CG says that Lutheran traditions are the cause of the problem and must be changed. Confessionalists declare that the trend is the result of cultural forces that never have been, are not now, and never will be friendly to the Christian church. Faithfulness to our theology is required, not retreat from it, while still reaching out in any way we can without giving in to a secular culture.

CG holds up the Great Commission as the sole measure of effectiveness.[7] CG measures growth quantitatively in terms of attendance and qualitatively in terms of the members' (customers') involvement. Research and analysis of these measures determines the prescription for repair and growth. The evidence, they say, is staring us in the face:

> We are a dying church. The average age of Missouri members is 55 by conservative estimates, far higher than the average age of our nation. At the same time, there is no growth in younger membership. Catastrophic membership decline is, therefore, on the horizon as these older members begin to die. Even though the Synod has expended millions of dollars over the past five years, the Synod is in membership decline.[8]

Kent Hunter says: "Jesus with His missionary mind-set, what we call Church Growth eyes, has a great concern that the presentation of the Gospel and the Word of God be effective."[9] To accomplish this mission, CG advocates one thing: change. This change will be brought about by transforming "style" but not "substance." According to David Luecke, "The distinction between substance and style is really an invitation to discuss where, in this period of cultural change, the line can be drawn between what can change in church life and what cannot. What's inside the line remains unchangeable substance; what's outside the line is style that can change."[10]

The agent of change is marketing. Pastors, District and Synod executives, and lay leaders flock to church-marketing workshops and seminars. Hunter is a regular participant in the numerous CG workshops offered by Community Church of Joy in Glendale, Arizona.[11] There, attendees learn to become "customer oriented." This is held up as the cure for declining congregations and synods such as the LCMS. Walt Kallestad writes:

> In the for-profit community, quality is measured by the customer, and quality means meeting or exceeding the customer's expectations 100 percent of the time. The same definition may be used for quality in ministry. It means meeting or exceeding the expectations or needs of the customer in such a way as to fully satisfy him or her, and to do it in a manner without deficiencies.[12]

Hunter explains his diagnostic process: Step one: "The issue of analysis is the issue of evaluation. Christians who are serious about the work of the Lord and take responsibility for being good stewards of the mysteries of God will evaluate their performance and the effectiveness of the church's ministry."[13] Step two: "The Church Growth Movement has designed an investigative ministry that looks at the diseases congregations can experience.... The ministry discipline of diagnosis is coupled with prescription suggesting what congregations can do to remove the roadblocks so that God can be God in and through the church most effectively."[14] Step three: "[Strategic thinking] is a deliberate and intentional effort to harness the resources available to the church and to choose priorities that clearly have the most impact in light of the objective of the Great Commission."[15]

Confessional Lutherans have to live with the same declining membership statistics, but they vigorously disagree with the CG diagnosis. CG has a bias against Lutheran practices, which it labels as tradition, style, and adiaphora. But these cannot be modified without changing the substance, the theological foundation, the Gospel. As the Church Growth Study Committee's report concludes:

> The problems with the Church Growth Movement have to do with the assumption that God's Word is not sufficient, that it needs to be supplemented with "contempo-

rary social and behavioral sciences." In practice, this means changing the church—its worship, its self-understanding, and its confession—so that it conforms to contemporary American culture. Marketing techniques turn sinners in need of salvation into consumers. The church adapts its practices to attract consumers and seeks thereby to grow in numbers. Institutes and mega-church workshops and church-growth materials are potential sources of introducing alien doctrines into the life and mission of the Synod. Tragically, the Gospel itself is sometimes compromised, redefined, or treated as secondary.[16]

Confessional Lutherans agree with CG's request for attention to things like adequate parking and the use of modern technology when appropriate. But CG's basic remedy is opposed to the means of real change: the Word of God. We need faithfulness to the means of grace. We need to reach out to an anti-Christian, postmodernist culture with the same defenses and offenses the church has used throughout the centuries: catechesis, evangelism, and discipleship.[17]

Furthermore, Confessionalists declare that the CG movement has succumbed to the cultural pressures of pragmatism and success at all costs. For example, notice the title of one CG book: *Courageous Churches: Refusing Decline, Inviting Growth.*[18] The authors present no biblical or Lutheran Confessional material that substantiates such a principle. To refuse any decline and do whatever it takes to grow—these are modern marketing principles. God certainly invites growth, but decline sometimes happens. Scripture prophecy in the New Testament predicts declining faith in the end times. Jesus Himself said: "However, when the Son of Man comes, will He find faith on the earth?"(Luke 18:8b). In CG words, "When Christ returns, will He find a vibrant, reproducing people?" The danger here is that as we approach that true Last Day, we become focused on growth in numbers instead of being alert in prayer and strong in faith.[19] Suffering will be the certain plight of Christ's people during the last days. They are to expect this. The church will not be a huge attraction to the multitudes of the secular culture. Because they can only enter through the "narrow gate" (Matthew 7:13, 14), their number will be few. David H. Scaer comments on this correlation:

> The Sermon (Matthew 7:13–14) and the Lucan parallel (13:24) are the only places where the word "narrow" is used. The word suggests that requirements of the Sermon with its prescribed limitations demand adherence without wavering. The word for "hard" means more literally the way marked by tribulations. Thus the stress of the Christian religion is less on its moral conduct and more on the suffering of the community of the followers of Jesus for his sake.[20]

The Synod in convention in 1995 passed a resolution declaring that just because a congregation was plateaued or declining, this was not necessarily any indication of spiritual disease or lack of interest in lost souls. The resolution went on to refute those in CG who would equate growth with God's blessings in every case. CG is primarily interested (as the evidence shows) in growth at any cost. To do this, CG has accommodated Lutheran theology to alien theologies. Effectiveness and accountability derive from a business mind-set that always looks to the bottom line. CG has sold out to such a marketing orientation. Its views about the health, diseases, and remedies for congregations that are not demonstrating a "mission orientation" are unacceptable. In CG, faithfulness to God's Word is overshadowed by this urgency to change and multiply.

Critiquing CG on this, Douglas Webster points out:

> Churches striving for excellence do not necessarily translate that concern into meaningful Communion services, consistent church discipline, training in spiritual disciplines, better premarital preparation or more Christ-centered worship. The excellence they seek is, by

definition and perception, a quality separate from godliness. A market-driven church in pursuit of excellence may have a very efficient management team, but little heart for world missions. . . . Church marketers do not say that the church can be successful apart from the work of the Holy Spirit and prayer, but they create that impression by defining excellence in terms foreign to the New Testament and familiar to the marketplace.[21]

The Church Growth Study Committee calls this misleading, worldly measurement of effectiveness "spiritually harmful" to the church, listing the following harmful conditions:

When spiritual life is measured in terms of happiness, earthly success and appearance, worldly wisdom and human glory (1 Corinthians 1:21–25); When behavioral and social sciences are given a shared authority with the Word of God as a measure of spiritual truth; When it is thought that saving faith can be imparted by human market strategies or that the growth of the Holy Christian Church can be adequately or accurately measured by numbers (Matthew 7:13–14, 16:18; Acts 2:47; Colossians 2:19); When a congregation sees itself as necessarily more faithful because it is not growing, or, conversely, when a congregation views growing numbers and income as an indication that Christ is necessarily building His church. Numbers, large or small, are not a litmus test of the Gospel's power (Matthew 7:24–27); When anything other than faithfulness by pastor or people to the pure Gospel and Sacraments of Christ is used to measure the "health of a congregation" (1 Corinthians 2:2).[22]

A FINAL THOUGHT

The "bottom line" is fundamental to continued existence for both a business and a church. However, each must define the bottom line differently. Businesses monitor the bottom line and intensively research, plan, implement, and modify their activities to enhance it. Churches that imitate this managerial model end up focusing on the one variable that no one is able to control: conversion. Saving a soul is out of our control.

Our bottom line is our accountability to the faithful proclamation of the precious Gospel. As Jesus said to the Pharisee Nicodemus: "You should not be surprised at this! The Holy Spirit saves wherever it pleases, when it pleases. You do not know where it begins, or where it goes next" (John 3:1–8, paraphrased).

There has been deception among us that must come to an end. The deception is twofold: first, that God's means of grace are not effective in saving whom He pleases, when He pleases. A fellow pastor told of the disappointment he experienced in his seminary field work when his supervising pastor exclaimed, "Law and Gospel just doesn't cut it with the people anymore!" That is, in today's tough church market, God needs a little help. CG adherents gather around their consultants and seminar leaders to hear of new techniques that, when "effectively and enthusiastically" embraced and implemented, will cause the church to grow. Conversions will happen if CG principles are utilized. The bottom line becomes the only objective.

This is where the second deception enters. For all its frenetic activity, CG received poor marks during the last decade of the twentieth century. One research expert summarizes: "Claims of prolific church growth have been grossly exaggerated; not only are most churches not increasing in size, but those that are expanding are doing so at the expense of other churches. More than 80 percent of the adults who get counted as new adherents and thus as part of the growth statistic are really just transplants from other churches—religious consumers in search of the perfect, or at least more exciting or enjoyable, church experience. Disturbingly little church growth is attributable to new converts. All in all, it was not a good decade for church growth."[23]

My hat goes off to David Luecke for coming forward in print to declare:

> There is a difference between observing, on the one hand, that most growing churches have certain characteristics and claiming, on the other hand, that most churches with those characteristics will grow. That difference is the unpredictable Holy Spirit, who will not be confined to a set of techniques. . . . Ten years later I know more but also less about church growth than I did before. . . . I know less about techniques that work because everything I tried worked a little, but none worked a lot. I know more about dependence on God for His blessings on church growth efforts. [24]

While we can affirm Luecke in this discovery and humble admission, we still have great concern with his conclusions and advice from these experiences: "The Holy Spirit still does his work through specific personalities and through what looks a lot like happenstance. . . . While church leaders cannot on their own produce an infectious church spirit, they need to be good stewards to avoid turning one off."[25] This is the same logic the government uses to justify pouring more money into failed programs.

Where does CG turn when the bottom line is not what it is supposed to be when CG principles are followed? What is at stake here is the Gospel. The bottom-line mentality and techniques brought into the church from the outside disciplines of management, marketing, and sociology have caused the whole perspective of church health and Gospel purity to be questioned, challenged, changed, and abandoned. Confessional Lutherans insist with St. Paul that this places the people back under the Law. It is not Lutheran. It is not biblical. We cannot stand on it. We need to be faithful stewards of the mysteries of God. Our Confession states it clearly:

> So that we may obtain this faith, the ministry of teaching the gospel and administering the sacraments was insti-

tuted. For through the Word and the sacraments as through instruments the Holy Spirit is given, who effects faith where and when it pleases God in those who hear the gospel, that is to say, in those who hear that God, not on account of our own merits but on account of Christ, justifies those who believe that they are received into grace on account of Christ. Galatians 3:14b: "So that we might receive the promise of the Spirit through faith." They condemn the Anabaptists and others who think that the Holy Spirit comes to human beings without the external Word through their own preparations and works. (AC V)

6

WILL THE PEOPLE PERISH?

CHURCH GROWTH CLAIM:

When church workers approach their task as defenders of the truth without adding the concept of sharing the truth, they abdicate responsibility of leadership.... They fail to cast (communicate) vision. As the proverb says, "Where there is no vision, the people perish."[1]

CONFESSIONAL LUTHERAN CLAIMS:

[If] Lutherans are to be contagious in their faith, they need to be convincing and therefore convinced as Lutherans—not as imitation Pentecostalists, imitation "Evangelicals," or imitation anything else. Such convictions cannot be "put on" as salesmanship bravado. They arise quite naturally, or I should say, supernaturally, from faithful preaching, faithful catechesis, faithful sacramental life, and faithful pastoral care—all upheld within the mutual solidarity of a faithful, confessionally sound congregation. Such a fount of conviction will draw others into the fold, the members' own life and confession being the chief "cutting edge."[2]

When Moses went up on Mount Sinai to receive the Ten Commandments, the Israelites built the golden calf and then "sat down to eat and drink and got up to indulge in revelry. . . . The people were running wild" (Exodus 32:6, 25). That's the kind of thing that happens where God's revelation is absent (verse 18). People will get out of control and lose themselves in self-indulgence. As the Bible loses its influence across our land, we see that sort of lawlessness taking place.[3]

TOP PRIORITY

Citing Proverbs 29:18 ("Where there is no vision, the people perish," KJV), CG claims "vision" as a pastor's top priority in how to grow the church. Confessionalists counter that the proverb addresses what happens to a church or a society when it does not have and follow God's revelation.

CG utilizes Proverbs 29:18 as a slogan for visionary leadership by the pastor. The verse becomes a "strategy for outreach."[4] In essence, this means having a marketing plan for the church.[5] CG insists: "The reality is that every church is engaged in marketing. The only real questions are (1) what a church will call its marketing efforts, and (2) how good a job the church will do at marketing."[6] Furthermore, CG interprets "perish" in the verse as meaning "declining or plateaued membership." This ties in with understanding "vision" as the marketing outreach plan. A church should concentrate its resources on the outreach cycle: research, plan, implement, feedback, and modify. If not, it will eventually become defunct. In other words, either get "CG eyes" or you will be a thing of the past.

Businesses utilize the "vision statement" as the driving force behind every decision. This becomes the touchstone that everyone should embrace for the long-term health and security of the organization. The leadership at the top is responsible for its conception, communication, and constant monitoring and maintenance. The vision statement should not be a "static" document, but a live, working, dynamic instrument that reflects the markets, the customer needs, and the company's resultant efforts to satisfy these needs and capture market share.

The CG movement has brought such an understanding of "vision" into the realm of the church. Feeling the pressures and needs expressed by existing and potential members, pastors have felt unprepared and untrained to provide "visionary" leadership. In many congregations, laypeople in active roles have training and experience with managerial/marketing leadership; this creates pressure for pastors.

Noted CG advocate Stephen Hower suggests that leadership principles can be adapted from nonbiblical fields of expertise, because these same principles are exemplified in the Bible:

> Effective leadership, like Christian values, is more often caught than taught. It is my hope that, through the example of [the famous men and women that Hower writes about], readers will gain inspiration and motivation that will better equip them for their role as a Christian influence in the kingdom of the Lord. Not all the character sketches are about well-known Christians. Some of the men and women, it might be argued, were not Christian at all. Each character study does, however, provide insight into a godly character trait substantiated in Scripture and useful for study. There is value in the lessons successful leaders have learned if only through the observation of God's natural principles at work. There is eternal value when those principles are applied by Christians to promote the saving Gospel of the one Savior, Jesus Christ.[7]

As one CG compilation puts it, "Whatever else is involved in the transition to a courageous church, . . . pastoral leadership is crucial. Clergy must be leaders, not only theologians and pastors. They keenly affect the mix or implementation of principles that provides for positive change."[8]

At the heart of this leadership is the desire for positive change using a body of principles that CG provides. The book *Courageous Churches: Refusing Decline, Inviting Growth* provides an excellent opportunity to read comments on these principles from LCMS pastors and their congregations.

One central CG principle is the implementation of a vision statement. This mission, outreach-oriented dream of how the church needs to be changed is vital to the success of all the other principles. Many LCMS pastors admit that this is at the heart of their ministry. For example, Pastor John Kieschnick of Houston, Texas, describes his use of this principle: "All I really had to do was help the people of Gloria Dei organize their vision with reality" (91).

A second principle is openness to new ideas. This is based primarily on the foundational CG notion of growth through meeting people's needs, doing whatever it takes, wherever, by whomever. 1 Corinthians 9:19–21 provides the supposed biblical basis for this restlessness with what is not working. Rev. Elmer Thyr of California comments: "I subscribe to everything that anybody is putting out, trying to improve on what I'm doing" (92).

A third principle is actively promoting change for more growth in Christ's kingdom. This begins with the pastor; then the leadership must embrace change and, finally, the people. Rev. Robert Brown explains his first engagement with this CG leadership tenet when he first arrived at an Evansville, Indiana, congregation: "I asked them this one question: Do you want to grow? They said yes. I said, okay, this is how we do it. We started to make the changes immediately" (94). There's always room for improvement in quality and effectiveness in meeting needs, so this CG principle seems always pertinent. The current business best-seller *Who Moved My Cheese?*[9] is widely touted by CG as a marvelous literary illustration of this principle.

As these principles are put into practice, another principle comes into play: the CG pastor must lead the people to take risks. Typically, CG pastors speak of building when finances are lacking or being willing to "accept criticism from other churches, area pastors, or the denomination" for trying new outreach, worship, or community ministry projects (95). Rev. Michael Gibson of California goes so far as to say: "We're willing to fail for the purpose of reaching other people with the Gospel. And we do fail occasionally; but that's okay, because we really celebrate our successes" (96).

CG also admonishes pastors to practice leadership that centers on "equipping people for ministry rather than just ministering to people" (99). This is truly a significant piece of the growth puzzle. It is a major change from the traditional role that pastors have played in congregational life. It not only changes their orientation from inside (focus on the congregation) to outside (outreach to the lost), but it also contends that laypeople are ministers too. Some pastors are so committed to this concept of "everyone a minister" that they call their elders to a lifelong commitment, similar to that of ordained ministers (100–1). According to this principle, what used to be a clear distinction between pastors and laypeople is seen as detrimental to growth.

When these leadership principles are utilized, one should expect conflict. CG addresses this: conflict must be dealt with positively. This entails three strategies: ignore when it is helpful to do so, but confront when called for; do not let conflict occupy much of the pastor's agenda; and realize that everyone will not accept the CG style of leadership. Primarily this relates to other pastors who do not yet adhere to CG methodology and to laypeople who will not adapt to change. As Pastor Jeffrey King of Massachusetts says, "One pastor called what I was doing 'McWorship,' like McDonalds. I thought about it and came to the conclusion that that was really a great compliment.

Who attracts more people than McDonalds? If we can present Christ and our confessional beliefs in a way that would attract as many people as McDonalds, that would be tremendous" (104).

Although CG pastoral leadership involves both task-oriented leadership and people-oriented leadership, CG leaders "display task-oriented behaviors because mission itself is goal-oriented" (105). Because the goal is to reach the unchurched, CG is prepared to let unhappy congregational members depart rather than abandon task-oriented leadership. Walt Kallestad, at a 1988 CG conference in Phoenix, said that he had to get rid of the 15 percent of grumpy Lutherans in his congregation before he could make progress.

In a remarkable summation of their leadership principles, advocates of CG insist that they strive to avoid the biblical shepherd model of leadership since it leads to flock preservation and maintenance. CG mission/vision-oriented leadership favors planning and equipping the sheep to shepherd themselves and other sheep.[10]

THE GOSPEL NEEDS NO SUPPLEMENTS!

The CG interpretation of Proverbs 29:18 is unbiblical. Their leadership principles are driven by business models while rejecting the biblical model that traditional churches correctly use. If their key leadership principle is opposed to the biblical faith, then all that derives from it is corrupt as well. CG presents a modified gospel, a different gospel, a damnable thing rather than the saving power of God.

The word for "vision" in Proverbs 29:18 is the Hebrew *chazon*.[11] This cannot be equated with an outreach strategic plan, but rather refers to "divine communication in a vision, oracle, prophecy."[12] That is, the Word of God. "Perish" here does not mean "decline," but "cast off restraint."[13] Ironically,

the advocates of CG, as they interpret Bible passages—
Proverbs 29:18 being but one—often cast off restraint. They
are not careful handlers of God's Word and the Lutheran Confessions.[14]

This lack of proper biblical interpretation and application has led the CG movement to become dominated by disciplines outside the realm of theology. Many of the good
laypeople in LCMS pews understand management, marketing,
and leadership techniques. However, when pastors impose
these business models on Christ's church, it begs the question:
"What does the Lord mean by 'being in the world, but not of
the world'?" Note the protest over the impact on the Gospel:

> Some emphases of the Church Growth Movement have
> highlighted the importance of mission work and a desire
> for healthy growth. There is certainly nothing wrong
> with common sense suggestions . . . The problems with
> the Church Growth Movement have to do with the
> assumption that God's Word is not sufficient, that it
> needs to be supplemented with "contemporary social
> and behavioral sciences." In practice, this means chang-
> ing the church—its worship, its self-understanding, and
> its confession—so that it conforms to contemporary
> American culture. Marketing techniques turn sinners in
> need of salvation into consumers. The church adapts its
> practices to attract consumers and seeks thereby to grow
> in numbers. Institutes and mega-church workshops and
> church-growth materials are potential sources of intro-
> ducing alien doctrines into the life and mission of the
> Synod. Tragically, the Gospel itself is sometimes com-
> promised, redefined, or treated as secondary."[15]

Even some Baptist scholars have reacted to this danger:

> We believe that the issue is not simply whether market-
> ing principles and techniques can be used effectively to
> draw "unchurched" people to a worship service or to cre-
> ate a support group for men with midlife crises, as com-
> mendable as these activities might be. The more

> fundamental issue concerns the impact a marketing organization has on the church's self-understanding and mission. Put as starkly as we know how, the question is, Can the market-driven church remain Christ's church?[16]

They go on to express concern that the CG movement is distorting the church's mission by practicing marketing and techniques that undermine the Gospel.[17]

To buy into the marketing orientation locks pastors into a mode that assumes the means of grace are not efficacious of themselves, but need to be constantly evaluated, modified, reevaluated, enhanced, repackaged, and researched to see if the almighty consumer—the unchurched person—is buying into it. This is very dangerous and can be spiritually harmful, if not fatal. Style cannot be separated from substance. As the Bible declares, "Don't you know that a little yeast works through the whole batch of dough?" (1 Corinthians 5:6).

The Good Shepherd charges his under-shepherds to provide good pasture (pure teaching) for the flock and to watch out for predators (false teachers). A good pastor should not become obsessed with teaching sheep to care for sheep (see Psalm 23; Isaiah 56; Ezekiel 34; John 10).

GET IT OUT, BUT KEEP IT STRAIGHT!

Certainly the church must not shirk its task to reach out with the Good News to unbelievers. Here the shepherd/sheep imagery is most helpful: "Does he not leave the ninety-nine in the open country and go after the lost sheep until he finds it?" (Luke 15:4).

As Dr. Barry said so aptly: "Doctrine and evangelism are wedded in the history of the early church. This union lies embedded, for example, in the book of Acts. Let no one put asunder what God has joined together!"[18] Our sainted LCMS

President was a fervent advocate of getting out the Good News about Jesus Christ crucified for sins. He urged not just

> giving ourselves a pep talk. For, in the end, it will not be pep talks that cause the outreach that has been going on for centuries in the history of the Christian church. This kind of effort cannot be sustained for so long a period of time on pep talks. There is something about the gospel message itself that simply will not stay contained. It reaches out to all people, no matter who they may be, and draws them in.[19]

This pure Gospel, without packaging or retooling, is still powerful to save both Jew and Gentile (Romans 1:16). The doctrine of justification by grace, for Christ's sake, through faith, must dominate, for it is substance and style rolled up in one. Challenging many of the CG claims concerning a marketing-oriented mission, Dr. Barry wrote:

> Finally, the doctrine of justification by God's grace becomes a norm for evangelism within the larger setting of the normative Scriptures. I find it interesting that in the Acts 15 council, mission to the Gentiles was evaluated in two ways. Peter pointed out that it went hand-in-glove with justification by grace for Christ's sake through faith, and James showed that it was in accord with the Scriptures. So, in our day, we can ask: in our various outreach efforts, are we remaining faithful to the great truth of justification by grace? It is too good to be true, but it is true! And are we standing on the Scriptures? There is no way we can consider the audience—not the message—to be sovereign.[20]

Dr. Barry cited Luther to show that when care is not taken in evangelism to discern error in regards to this central doctrine, the saving Gospel becomes contaminated.[21] The CG emphasis on growth alone ignores the biblical admonition to maintain purity of doctrine for the sake of salvation. The influence of American Evangelicalism has corrupted the Lutheran understanding and practice of evangelism, disengaging the close Lutheran relationship of doctrine and outreach. Dr. Barry noted, "To reclaim a Lutheran view of evangelism we will perhaps need to change the way we perceive the evangelistic challenge and the ways we meet it."[22]

A FINAL THOUGHT

I cannot fault CG for its fervent desire to seek and save the lost. However, I must ask, Do you give up anything in this rush to grow, to succeed, to be relevant, to please the customer? The evidence convinces me that the answer must be yes. CG gives up the purity of the Gospel and the correct administration of the Sacraments in its zeal to grow.

As Dr. Barry observed, the need for balance between outreach and doctrine cannot be avoided. If the object is to grow by all means, at all costs, then CG should be equally focused on maintaining pure doctrine. Their writings show well-meant assertions that they are doing such. But fervent dedication to a cause can blind one to realities. It has been my experience in reading and listening to CG advocates that they are not apt handlers of God's Word or the Confessions. They reduce doctrine to a "barrier" that the Gospel cannot overcome. Sincere pastors spend their time not protecting their sheep from predatory false doctrine or providing the green pastures of pure teaching, but rather in cheerleading and coaching. They try get the sheep to shepherd the lost sheep. In fact, by means of church marketing, they get the sheep to lead the shepherd.

This manufactured need for "vision"—really just marketing strategy and not God's revelation—is joined with the false notion that if "vision" is not the main thrust, then the congregation will decline. The true vision of God's Word exhorts us rather to be faithful to God's means of grace while seeking every opportunity to proclaim the Good News to everyone.

7

EVERYONE A MINISTER?

CHURCH GROWTH CLAIMS:

There are those who talk about the office of the ministry as if it is a very clear, detailed, biblically described concept. In fact, the New Testament has a lot to say about the *function* of ministry, some reflection on the *roles* of ministry and less to say on the *office* of ministry. Oscar Feucht, in his outstanding book *Everyone a Minister*, has thoroughly treated this concept of the priesthood of all believers. . . . The role of ministry, on the other hand, is the position in ministry for those who are involved. These are people who are in leadership positions and are primarily dedicated to equipping people for ministry.[1]

Better Recognition That Everyone Is A Minister . . . Growing churches today are learning how to organize more informally around giftedness rather than formally around positions and credentials. Inevitably this approach relies heavily on lay ministry. Lutherans have two traditions of ministry. The narrow one keeps the authority and responsibility for ministry focused on the credentialed pastor. The broad one spreads the tasks of ministry widely among lay people, with the pastor functioning more as teacher and coach.[2]

CONFESSIONAL LUTHERAN CLAIMS:

Walther and the Missouri Synod said that the Office of the Ministry has its origin in its divine institution by Jesus Christ with the call of the apostles. The keys that pastors administer as bearers of the Office are the same keys Christ first gave to His church and to all members of the church. Pastors employ these keys, by God's command, as a matter of public responsibility. This remains the position of The Lutheran Church—Missouri Synod. . . . I would like to comment briefly on two basic trends that impact Church and Ministry, especially in the United States. These trends have helped shape the challenges presently faced by the Missouri Synod, and perhaps other church bodies too. The two trends are radical equality—the desire to put everyone on the same level—and individualism. . . . Whenever church life is seen largely to consist of persuading loosely-associated individuals to pull together in the same direction, the Office of the Ministry cannot help but be affected.[3]

In typical Church Growth thinking all are ministers, using their particular "gifts." The task of "pastor" or leading minister then is to choreograph the services of his (or her!) fellow-ministers with their various "gifts," and to provide a coordinating "vision." The office now is basically one of prodding, not one of distributing the saving Gospel treasures. Its character has changed from an *evangelical* to a *legal* institution, with a totally different understanding of the Gospel. A steward of God's mysteries is one thing—a CEO quite another.[4]

When the modern concept "everyone a minister" is equated with the priesthood of all believers: (a) This denies the true priesthood of all believers, which is exercised not only in worship and prayer, but also in daily vocation (i.e., the work of one's earthly calling, Christian witness in daily life, parental teaching in the home, etc.)

(1 Peter 2:9; Romans 12:1–2); (b) It confuses individual Christian lives with public offices in the church (Acts 6); (c) It can be used to undermine Jesus' gift of the office of preaching the Word and administering the Sacraments (pastoral office). (Ephesians 3:7–10; 4:11; 1 Corinthians 12:28–9; Augsburg Confession V, XIV, XXVIII [8])[5]

FUNCTION! FUNCTION! FUNCTION!

One can see the all-too-apparent disparity in attitudes concerning this doctrine of the church. There is a substantial gulf between the two positions concerning who a minister is and what a minister is to be. CG proclaims that Lutherans have been wrong in their traditional distinction between clergy and laity, and that this distinction needs to be removed so that true ministry and the growth of Christ's kingdom may occur. Confessionalists insist that the CG opinion is not Lutheran or biblical, but has been brought into our midst through outside theologies that are opposed to what the ancient church has always believed, confessed, and practiced. This particular discussion about the relationship between the Office of the Public Ministry and the priesthood of all believers continues to be, as one noted Lutheran puts it, "persistent and notorious."[6]

In CG, mobilizing the laity to greater service is vital. Although Kent Hunter speaks of an office of the ministry, he insists that this is not clearly explained in Scripture. What is clear, he says, is what the ministry's role is to be: to cast the vision for shared ministry and to equip the laity for their ministries. This equipping of everyone for ministry occurs through the discovery and development of spiritual gifts. This is critical, as Hunter states:

> The key to multiplication ministry and the mobilization of God's people is the God-given strategy of providing Christians with spiritual gifts. . . . There is an important distinction concerning spiritual gifts based on one's per-

ception of the primary purpose of the church. If the driving motive is to keep control of the church, and the confessional priority is an end in itself, then the gifts of the Spirit are threatening and of little value. But this is not so when the mission mind-set, an evangelical posture, generates a confessing church in which confessional standards are a means to an end.[7]

Therefore, CG views the pastoral office as "functional." This flows out of the primary function of equipping the sheep to go and minister to goats that Christ may make into sheep (Ephesians 4). According to Hunter, "This process of equipping the saints is the primary objective of making disciples."[8] He explains that this is critical,

> because it represents the key dynamic of multiplication. Multiplication is the key to world evangelization. . . . The ultimate goal of Church Growth is not growth, but the explosion of growth. What God intends is exponential growth, which takes place by multiplication. This does not or cannot happen when ministry is left to be conducted by the pastor. Such a view of the pastoral ministry turns a shepherd into a chaplain in the poorest sense of the word: a hireling for religious functionalism. The biblical way is that disciples are raised up and equipped to make disciples. The Great Commission says, "Go and make disciples." A disciple, by definition, is one who can multiply himself or herself.[9]

SOME TO SHEPHERD, OTHERS TO BE SHEPHERDED

Kurt Marquart counters that the Bible teaches just the opposite about the Office of the Public Ministry. He provides a list of New Testament texts and says, "Some are to feed, and some are to be fed, some to shepherd, others to be shepherded" (see John 21:15–17; 1 Peter 5:2; Acts 20:28; 1 Timothy 2:2, 4:16).[10] He claims that the directive in the Great Commission was not to all believers of the royal priesthood, but to those eleven called by Christ to carry on the prophetic office.[11] Marquart states:

> The watershed issue is this: is there in Christ an objective treasure-store of forgiveness, life, and salvation, to be offered, pressed upon, and actually handed out to needy sinners in preaching, absolution, Baptism, and in the Supper of the Lord's own most holy body and blood? If the answer is yes, then these holy means of salvation will absolutely shape and dominate the church's whole life, worship, and mission. "Therefore everything in the Christian church is so ordered that we may daily obtain full forgiveness of sins through the Word and through signs appointed to revive our consciences as long as we live" (*Large Catechism*, Creed, 55). And if all this is real, it requires a public service, the Gospel ministry, to carry it out in the name of Christ and His church.[12]

It is dumbfounding that those in the CG movement claiming to have Lutheran theological substance reject this central tenet of Lutheran theology and choose the unbiblical view of sheep-to-sheep ministry. Marquart exclaims:

> No! The Lord said not, "Organize My sheep into work-brigades, to do the real ministry themselves," but, "Feed My lambs, feed My sheep"! The shepherds are there precisely to "do ministry for the sheep," that is, to preach the Gospel and administer the sacraments to them. The church is not a self-service buffet. The shepherding Gospel ministry is there precisely to "reproduce" and nourish the sheep: "And how shall they believe in him of whom they have not heard?" asks St. Paul, and continues, "And how shall they hear without a preacher? And how shall they preach except they be sent?" (Romans 10:14, 15) That is just the logic of Augsburg Confession V: "In order that we may obtain [alone-justifying, Art. IV] faith, the ministry of teaching the Gospel and administering the sacraments was instituted."[13]

WHICH THEOLOGICAL MODEL DO YOU FOLLOW?

The CG position on ministry is flawed by leaning away from the Lutheran theological base to other, non-Lutheran models or paradigms.

> As there are basically only three great confessions, or versions of the Gospel in the West—the Roman Catholic, the Lutheran, and the Reformed or Calvinist—so there are three corresponding paradigms of the Ministry. Everything else is variation on these basic themes. . . . At the heart of the Roman Catholic position, usually labeled as "traditionalism," is a hierarchical structure of ministry, deacons, presbyters, and bishops. On the other hand is the Reformed or Calvinist position, typically referred to as "biblicalism," which is oriented towards church government and organization controlling the ministry. In between these two models lies the Lutheran position, which is called "mediating." Marquart puts it well: "the Church of the Augsburg Confession simply treasures the divine gift of the one apostolic Gospel-Preaching Office, that St. Paul defines as the stewardship of the Divine Mysteries" (1 Corinthians 4:1). [14]

Given this threefold approach, Marquart charges the Lutheran CG movement with abandoning the Lutheran middle position for the extreme of the Reformed-Calvinistic position.[15] He offers this Lutheran corrective: "(1) the priesthood of all and the ministry of some; (2) the one God-given Gospel-Ministry or Preaching Office, and various auxiliary offices established by the church; and (3) the two realms or governments, the spiritual and the temporal."[16]

THE PRIESTHOOD OF ALL
AND THE MINISTRY OF SOME?

Luther's reestablishment of the biblical understanding of the priesthood of all believers serves as a major factor in the disagreement over the Public Ministry. As we have seen, CG proclaims "everyone a minister." The pastor is just a "functional" person (in the Reformed view of ministry) promoted from the ranks for the sake of order and organization/specialization. As many CG practitioners proclaim, the pastor is "a minister to the ministers."

Marquart declares this to be unbiblical and unlutheran, quoting the first LCMS president: "The spiritual priesthood is not a public office [*Amt*] in the church."[17] The rub, Marquart explains, is in the church's outreach:

> We are overwhelmed with a pragmatic clamor for successful methods, and with various sectarian schemes and even neo-Pentecostal fantasies about so-called "spiritual gifts" and the centrality of "meta-church" small groups. The question is not whether all Christians can and ought to confess their faith. Of course they do and must. The real question is whether in the church's official and intentional mission work, in the planting of churches, God's gift and institution for this very purpose is to be central.[18]

This brings us again to the center of one's theology. CG sees the center being "the absolute primacy of the missionary task, that is, the work of evangelizing non-Christians and incorporating them into living churches."[19] But CG puts this in opposition to the God-given Office of the Public Ministry through its called and ordained servants of the Word.

David Luecke says the Lutheran model of Public Ministry is only a German tradition, which hinders the Gospel's spread:

> The work done by traditionally called pastors is largely a matter of spiritual giftedness. The Apostle Paul teaches this. Then perhaps some gifted church leaders with minimal course training might function as well and even better than many who have extensive graduate-level education. This observation suggests a model different from the accepted practice of first training prospective

ministers in seminary and then having congregations engage them, often with disappointing results. A reasonable alternative is to have congregations first identify leaders of proven effectiveness in their midst and then bring them formal course work that can strengthen their ministry while they continue doing it.[20]

Hunter concurs:

The approach that one has concerning this issue of the priesthood of all believers greatly depends on the perspective from which one is coming. For example, when the church's main objective is to be confessional, the top priority may be expressed as "Here I stand." The temptation then is to be control-oriented and there is an overemphasis on the organizational structure of the church. This is expressed primarily in an overprotective position concerning the office of the ministry.[21]

Lutheran CG experts disagree with all three of Marquart's stated Lutheran principles of the Public Ministry. Hunter counters with his own: (1) the role of full-time ministers as equipping the rest of the ministers to evangelize; (2) the urgency of spiritual gifts; and (3) the multiplication principle of ministry.[22]

WILL THE REAL EPHESIANS 4:12 PLEASE STAND UP?

At the heart of this disagreement over Public Ministry is the understanding of Ephesians 4:12: "for the perfecting of the saints, for the work of the ministry" (KJV), "to prepare God's people for works of service" (NIV). CG agrees with the modern, paraphrased translation of this verse. However, if this is not the correct interpretation, much of their biblical basis for "equipping the ministers (laity)" evaporates.

Hunter casually quotes Ephesians 4:11–12, assuming the modern meaning:

These gifts [apostles, prophets, evangelists, pastors/ teachers] have been given to the church to equip God's saints so that they can do the work of ministry. This process of equipping the saints is the primary objective of making disciples. If the task of making disciples becomes an academic exercise, people will be taught and discipled simply so that they will learn more. If there is no other objective than to learn more, to gain more knowledge, this will lead to dead orthodoxy, traditional-ism, apathy, and fear in the body of Christ. No one will be willing to witness for fear of saying the wrong thing— conveying the wrong message.[23]

DIRECTION IS EVERYTHING

Luecke adds an important question to the discussion: from which direction is the Public Ministry coming? He answers that there are only two options: top down (called, ordained clergy in control) and bottom up (priesthood of believers in control).[24] He suggests that one can define the dif-ference simply. Top-down sees the "minister" as the one hold-ing that office, the one who preaches and administers the Sacraments to the believers. Bottom-up reserves the title of "minister" for the people—the priesthood of all believers— who have their God-given ministries to carry out.[25] This fits perfectly with a "marketing orientation" whereby the power to make product decisions is transferred from the company to the customer. But such orientation begs the question about authority, since a fervent CG pastor can be equally as "author-itarian" in his leadership style as any Confessional Lutheran.

Luecke sees the Lutheran tradition as unbiblical, since it holds to a "narrow view" that became dominant over Luther's "broad view." He asserts that this is an artifact from the seven-teenth century that persists today among Confessional Luther-ans.[26] He also sees the Lutheran practice of the divinely instituted Office of Public Minister as being the result of a failure to adhere to the biblical principles of Paul regarding spiritual gifts and the primary task of "the lead minister . . . to be a builder who equips the others to build up the fellowship that is their basic identity as a local congregation."[27]

Organizing around Spiritual Gifts

Both Luecke and Hunter bemoan the lack of proper biblical teachings from their Lutheran seminaries concerning spiritual gifts. They claim a biblical mandate to organize Christ's church around the spiritual gifts of all the ministers of God in Romans 12; Ephesians 4; and 1 Corinthians 12.

Hunter declares: "My personal experience with spiritual gifts parallels that of thousands of other Confessional Lutherans. It is an example of what happens when academia reigns and the church is more interested in defending the truth than sharing it with the world."[28] Luecke says: "The leadership task is to identify the giftedness of the members at hand and to get these various contributions employed so they can benefit all."[29] Hunter affirms that Confessional Lutherans will not find anything useful in spiritual gifts because their primary focus is not on missions. He makes the charge that Confessionalism is threatened by spiritual gifts because of the likely concomitant loss of ecclesiastical control. Hunter adds: "It takes a significant Christian self-confidence to allow God to be God and to operate His church the way He intends, out of our hands."[30] He believes that the gifts are to serve the Lord and His people, and that service and ministry are interchangeable words from the Greek to English.[31] "Therefore, one of the major responsibilities of key leaders and others who fill the role of ministry in Christian congregations is to guide and direct the priesthood of all believers to discover, develop, and use their spiritual gifts."[32]

What Is Primary?

Kurt Marquart strikes to the heart of things in his disagreement with CG's direction away from the power of God working in the Gospel purely preached and the Sacraments rightly distributed. He declares that CG basically gives lip service to stock phrases like "Word and Sacrament," "means of grace," and "pastoral office." Lutheran CG advocates sprinkle on this language habitually. The real question is what they mean by "ministry" and the "work of pastors." Marquart charges Lutheran CG with selling out to foreign theologies and Pentecostal influences such as that of the noted CG teacher C. Peter Wagner. Marquart cuts close to the true center:

> The notion of "spiritual gifts" is not (like Baptism!) an optional piece of "Church Growth" machinery. It functions in fact as a basic reference point and organizing principle. For Lutherans that pivotal place belongs to the pure preaching of the Gospel and the right administration of the sacraments—by rightly called ministers! In the nature of the case these positions are mutually exclusive. It is muddle-headed to try to salvage some "both/and" from the contradiction.[33]

After quoting CG professor C. Peter Wagner, Marquart then rightly rebukes him:

> "The gift of the evangelist is the special ability that God gives to certain members of the Body of Christ to share the gospel with unbelievers in such a way that men and women become Jesus' disciples and responsible members of the Body of Christ." If this definition is taken seriously, it entails the sacrilegious absurdity that Our Lord Himself lacked the "gift of evangelism," for instance when at Capernaum He refused to stroke His hearers' "felt needs," and "many of His disciples went back, and walked no more with Him" (John 6:66).[34]

Just as the CG advocates are true to their primary focus on evangelism, Marquart remains consistent with the Confessional insistence on pure Gospel: "The fundamental fallacy here—as in revivalism—is that the power to create faith, or at least the decisive part of that power, is attached not to the Gospel itself, as Scripture teaches (Luke 8:11; Romans 1:16, 10:17; Colossians 1:6; 1 Peter 1:23–25), but to the person of the proclaimer."[35]

THE CLEAVAGE OF THE OFFICE
FROM THE FUNCTION

This CG separation of the office and the function, claims Klemet Preus, "is a reflection of the two-tiered understanding of the church."[36] CG goals are not the issue, says Preus; the issue is theology.[37] CG interprets everything not through the Lutheran paradigm of pure Gospel, but through the CG paradigm of mission.

This is achieved, Confessionalists claim, by reading the paradigm into Scripture. This is especially true with the critical CG passage, Ephesians 4:12. Henry Hamann contends that modern Bible translations of this passage, especially RSV, TEV, and NIV, translate as the NEB does: "to equip God's people for work in His service." Such a faulty translation of the original Greek leads to this fundamental CG principle: "What is the pastor's job? To equip the saints (Ephesians 4:12). The church is to be a training ground for members of the body. They are to be guided by the pastor, their trainer."[38] Hamann shows through careful work with the relevant Greek words καταρτισμοσ and καταρτιζω, "prepare," that this popular translation is against all established and accepted grammatical understanding of these words. He charges in this regard:

> We are not concerned only with grammar and the proper use of words in this study. Even if that were all that is at stake, we could speak of a necessary correction. . . . It appears to me that what has really made the popular translation so popular is an underlying dogmatic position. To be quite blunt about it, lay people and those

who for one reason or another are anti-clerical see here a convenient text to support their point of view. (45)

He substantiates this charge by saying:

If a comma is put between the first two concepts, no doubt is left that the gift of the ministries has a double object; all the saints benefit from it, but only select ministers carry out the work of building the body. This interpretation has an aristocratic, that is, a clerical and ecclesiastical flavour; it distinguishes the (mass of the) "saints" from the (superior class of the) officers of the church. A clergy is now distinct from the laity, to whom the privilege and burden of carrying out the prescribed construction work are exclusively assigned.[39]

Hamann insists that Paul's words "do not carry implications of superiority, aristocracy, and lack of lay activity." And again, "What is wrong about being merely beneficiaries? Is that not the implication of the whole Gospel?" (46–47). This assumes that direction from above or direction from below are the only choices! Hamann explains: "But the idea of 'above' and 'below' does not at all fit the actual scheme of things, either in the church or in the state. There are different ministries, different forms of service. In a truly united people, faithful performance of what you can do is what counts, and status and rank do not enter into consideration at all" (48). Law and business intrude upon Karl Barth and the CG movement as well:

The church, according to Barth and many other writers on the subject, looks like a big business or a big corporation, with every person picked to do specific tasks that will contribute to the success of the whole venture. At the head are the brains of the whole enterprise, equipping the workers for their service for the whole. This explains the favour which phrases like "building the church" and "building the kingdom" enjoy. (48)

What the Bible describes is different. It shows God gathering His people around the means of grace, proclaimed and distributed by His pastors to the priesthood of all believers. Apart from these Divine Service gatherings, we see these priests going about their daily calls and vocations—parenting, marriage, career, recreation, friendships, and so on. Through these opportunities, this priesthood of believers shares their faith by their lives and by their confession of the living hope in them so that some might see their good works and faith and be brought out of spiritual darkness into the marvelous light of Christ.[40] As Hamann concludes:

> This is evangelization and church growth New Testament style. If a pastor aims at a congregation whose members live by faith active in love—which is the only thing that finally counts in Christ Jesus (Galatians 5:6)—and if he were sure that all his flock were doing just that, there would be no need at all for any further organization in his congregation beyond the barest minimum for the sake of order. There would be no stewardship and evangelization committees, no frantic searching and scratching of heads so that every member in the congregation would have something to do, no elaborate programs to show that everybody keeps busy in some spiritual activity. But there would be a mighty spiritual, churchly movement, as all members of the congregation would live their free lives of faith, loving their fellowmen, and serving them in freedom, heedless of self, as the whole body of Christ would grow and build itself up in love, each part doing its work. And that mighty spiritual movement would exert a tremendous attraction on the unbelieving world, as the Holy Spirit would, through it and the preached Word of the Gospel, add to the church daily those who were to be saved.[41]

A Final Thought

In business one always looks to improve activities so as to achieve success—always modifying strategy based on the changing market situation. But this should not be accepted in the church just because it works in other arenas. It should be evaluated based on God's Word solely. And we Lutherans use the Book of Concord to help us with our interpretation of God's Word.

When synodical and congregational membership declines or plateaus, how are we to react? Not by the unbiblical problem-solving approach taught in business colleges. Not by sociological analysis. Not by turning to theologies that are not faithful to all of God's Word. Not by concluding that people just don't like the Law/Gospel, means-of-grace emphasis that we have clung to as the only true way God will deal with us and give us real growth. The failure is not with God's Word, Law and Gospel, or the precious means of grace. The failure is with people, be they churched or unchurched. They do not like the things of God. Then why should we constantly rearrange and reorganize the church around their "felt needs"?

Some who say they are still Confessional Lutherans no longer believe that the Lutheran confession and means-of-grace ministry work. They say they do, and they write as though they do. But do they really? Do they practice it in their ministry? Do they try their very utmost to maintain and proclaim it in its purity? Do they trust it enough not to add or subtract anything from it? Do they still believe that it is sufficient to save the unchurched? Or do they believe that it must be supplemented?

At the root, they do not believe that the Office of the Public Ministry gives them the solution. So they junk the Lutheran confession and practice and adopt a bottom-up, people-oriented organization. Management studies from the corporate world seem to back them up. Christian denominations that have always believed in "function" over the Office of the Public Ministry will support them as well.

But Lutheran belief and practice and history will not allow this unbiblical intrusion. I can hear the protest already:

You're willing to accept decline; you don't want to strive and fight for growth. I reply: I'm willing to accept whatever response comes to God's holy means of grace. God will provide! His will be done, not mine or yours.

J. S. Bach said it well: "Sheep may safely graze and pasture, in a watchful pastor's eye." CG protests: That might have worked in an eighteenth-century flock. But not now! Twenty-first century sheep are smarter! We have our rights too, as priests! So no shepherd is going to tell us he's been sent by God, called and set aside to speak for God. We can show ourselves the way to good pasture and we can easily spot the predators that would threaten our flock without any shepherding. We sheep don't need any sheep-shepherd hierarchy. Bottom-up leadership is what we like and need.

I cannot help but admit my reaction to these CG Lutherans who have wandered so far from the faith. It ranges from amazement at their lack of interest in good exegesis and their apathy toward studying and practicing our Book of Concord to anger that they accommodate foreign theologies. Good biblical interpretation and application are sorely lacking in their thought. They admit they are pragmatists. They say the means of grace alone will not grow the church. There is no divine gift of the Office of the Public Ministry for them. There is no biblical understanding of the priesthood of all believers. Is it any wonder we have an incipient schism in our midst over this doctrine of the ministry? Lord, have mercy upon us!

8

WHERE DOES ONE GO FOR HELP?

CHURCH GROWTH CLAIMS:

Where should Lutheran church leaders look for concepts and advice on how to be and do church today? Scripture is, of course, the place to start. But where to look beyond the New Testament is increasingly at issue. . . . Unlike most Lutheran lay people and the minority of pastors committed to church growth, most Lutheran professors and professional church leaders seem to operate with something like disdain for those who in America are now called Evangelicals.[1]

Where pastors used to look to district and synod for program ideas, they now gather to learn from trend-setting congregations like Community Church of Joy in Phoenix or Willow Creek Community Church in the Chicago area. The consistent message of these teaching churches is that each congregation has to find its own way with what works best to accomplish its purpose in its own community. [2]

There is no doubt that the greatest influences on the Christian church since the Apostle Paul have been Martin Luther and Donald McGavran.[3]

CONFESSIONAL LUTHERAN CLAIMS:

Every criticism that the Lutherans over the centuries have applied to Pentecostalism and to enthusiasm can also be applied to the Church Growth Movement. The only difference is that the application has moved from the individual to the congregation and the church. . . . Kent Hunter's chief article of faith is "the mission paradigm." For him, those churches that do not use this paradigm are simply not pleasing to God. His ecclesiology is Pentecostalism gone corporate.[4]

McGavran and Wagner warmly endorse revivalism. The . . . definition of what it means to believe, given by McGavran and Win Arn, is a far cry from the biblical understanding of saving faith simply as God-given trust in His absolution. Instead, this Church Growth definition follows the familiar "decision" pattern of revivalism, as expounded above all by Charles Finney.[5]

LOOK TO PASADENA?

Where does one turn when in desperate need of aid in church work? One's answer reveals what one really trusts and believes in. As we have previously noted, the vast majority in the LCMS, of both the CG and Confessionalist persuasions, agree that there are important issues that need attention in our fellowship. Hardly anyone would declare that the situation is exactly what God or we would desire. However, there are sizeable differences over where one goes for help to remedy problems.

Some pastors in the LCMS look for help to Fuller Theological Seminary, Pasadena, California (so many that Fuller is sometimes called "our third seminary"). It was at this institution that Donald McGavran taught and first spread his teachings. The CG movement proclaims McGavran to be a God-sent leader to all of Christianity to lead us back to God's intended purpose: mission. Many LCMS pastors and leaders became students there and continue to look to Pasadena for answers.

Kent Hunter places McGavran even in such elite company as the apostle Paul and Martin Luther in terms of his timing and influence on the church.[6] He asserts this because the CG movement founded by McGavran has influenced so many churches and pastors in their thinking and practice. At a 1985 LCMS Minnesota South District conference, Hunter referred to CG as a new Reformation, not in theology but in practice.

Hunter and the CG movement believe the church has become bogged down by the academics in our seminaries and schools of higher learning. There we stress not the main focus of outreach to the unchurched, but rather nit-picking theological issues. Hunter stresses that he is not against good academic work. But he argues that there is an imbalance. As he puts it: "Academia becomes detrimental when it becomes the sole or supreme criterion for the functioning of the church."[7] To right this imbalance, CG recommends a heavy dosage of prescribed marketing, sociology, and management skills, as well as sitting at the feet of other church bodies. The need to do so is summarized by David Luecke: "Because of their different culture, Lutherans are prone to raise up Christ in ways that do not get the attention of people different from ourselves. The key is understanding and addressing needs they feel and recognize. Marketing is a modern term for the focus on trying to understand what potential consumers want when they are shopping to fill their needs."[8]

Thus, other denominations, which have begun utilizing the outside disciplines of marketing and sociology, have influenced LMCS pastors to consider using these disciplines in our church body. As Hunter confesses:

> Church Growth has taught me that, as a Lutheran, I have the freedom to reach the lost and that I can do it using different methods and numerous styles, and, simultaneously, have the unchanging Gospel, the condemning law, and the powerful means of grace as channels that change the eternal destiny of men and women. *I must confess that I am thrilled to be a Lutheran involved in Church Growth.* This is the best of both worlds: A commitment to sound biblical teaching as a Christian and sound biblical principles that help to get the Gospel out. You can identify and remove roadblocks that would hinder a clear transmission of that powerful good news.[9] (emphasis original)

In essence, the Lutheran church gives Hunter good doctrine but poor practice. Lutheranism does not give him a methodology to get this good doctrine communicated effectively to the saved and to the unchurched. Luccke equates this situation to the major departments in corporations, engineering and marketing:

> The Lutheran heritage is first-rate theological engineering that proclaims the Word of God in all its depth and breadth. If the Gospel were an automobile in the 1960s, Lutherans would be the Volkswagen of the industry. VW "beetles" were well-designed cars that were once well appreciated in America. The fact of the marketplace, however, is that Volkswagen lost considerable market share in this country in recent decades. Competitors paid more attention to features that car buyers grew to expect. Only in recent years have marketers been added to the engineer-dominated upper levels of VW corporate management. Their sales are now improving. Churches do not have to force choice between either engineering or marketing, between presenting theological expertise or innovatively addressing felt needs. The best is both/ and.[10]

Kurt Marquart responds that it is bad to allow such unlutheran theologies to be placed side-by-side with the Lutheran Confessions, imagining that one retains the Lutheran substance (engineering) with unlutheran style (marketing). To be able to do this, a Lutheran would have to believe "that 'Church Growth' itself is 'built on' the means of grace. It clearly is built on nothing of the sort."[11] Marquart comes to this conclusion based on the evidence he hears from Hunter and other LMCS CG advocates who pay lip service to the means of grace, but in the next breath praise revival theology. He provides an example of making prayer a means of grace. Korean Pentecostal minister Paul Yonggi Cho says:

> We emphasize that people should pray an hour every day. We urge them to come to church on Friday night. So they pray, and they repent of their sins, and their hearts are cleansed. This empowers them to come to the Lord and the church every Sunday morning. . . . When we pray, the Holy Spirit speaks to our hearts. We obey the word of the Holy Spirit. So prayer is very important. Through prayer we can repent of our sins, and through prayer we can hear the still, small voice of our Lord. Through prayer, people's hearts are cleansed, and they go running to their church without any guilt.[12]

LOOK TO GENEVA? TO AMSTERDAM?

What disturbs Marquart is that Hunter refers to Cho as "'a great expert on the relationship between prayer and church growth,' and concludes with thanks and a hearty 'God bless your work!'"[13] Marquart takes issue with such theology. This is just another instance of CGers who say they are Lutheran in substance but are in fact Finney-style revivalists. "At its Calvinistic best 'Church Growth' relies on the Reformed-pietistic direct encounter with the Spirit in prayer. At its Arminian (synergistic) worst, it projects a manipulative religious engineering, where everything depends on techniques and methods developed and certified as 'effective' by 'science.'"

Thus, Marquart protests that CG Lutherans spend time absorbing theologies that eventually may dominate and overwhelm what little Lutheran doctrine remains. They turn not to Lutheran sources for help (Wittenberg and its descendants, St. Louis and Ft. Wayne), but to Pasadena and Geneva, the spiritual home of the Reformed, or to Amsterdam, the spiritual home of the Arminians.

THERE'S NO PLACE LIKE A NEW-FOUND HOME

Lutheran CG practitioners do not deny that they are learning from non-Lutherans. They further proclaim that from these other groups, they learn how church and mission are to be carried out. Hunter, without reservation, even declares that there is a CG theology:

> There are those who like to say that Church Growth has no theology, that it is only methods and strategy. However, there are, clearly, three distinctive theological emphases that could form a systematic structure for understanding the doctrinal dimensions of Church Growth teaching. First of all, Church Growth is an ecclesiology. . . . Second, Church Growth is a study of stewardship. . . . Third, Church Growth is a missiology.[14]

Here, one can see that CG theology becomes preferred over Lutheran theology for LCMS practitioners in many areas: "In the area of ecclesiology, Church Growth teaches about prayer, spiritual warfare, and the diseases which churches can get, which, in turn, leads to the whole area of diagnostics."[15] Both prominent CG leaders in the Lutheran church (Luecke and Hunter) profess openly that they have been taught the true meaning of prayer not from the Lutheran church but from CG.[16] In fact, they say that Lutherans have been relying on the wrong thing for growth—faith in the Gospel—and not in the forms of prayer: intercessory prayer, strategic prayer, and warfare prayer. Hunter declares: "By this emphasis on prayer, Church Growth adherents acknowledge and demonstrate that God is the one who builds the church. It is a partnership in which the Lord expects His people to pray and to seek His direction."[17]

Hunter is representative of Lutheran CG advocates in not being able to discern Lutheran theology from alien theologies. Hunter admits his belief that prayer and ecclesiology are not shaped and directed by Lutheran theology, but rather corrected and informed by CG. Herman Sasse, a great Lutheran theologian, expressed his concern over just this sort of disengagement from the Lutheran Confessions in a 1951 essay:

> If it belongs to the essence of the Lutheran church that it is a confessional church, the church of the Unaltered Augsburg Confession—which in turn means, since the later confessions are all commentaries on the Augsburg Confession, the church of the Book of Concord—then it is a matter of the very existence of the Missouri Synod that it remain also in the future the church which is loyal to the Confession, rooted in the Confession, and proclaiming the evangelical truth attested by the Confession. It is a matter of her theological, not her physical existence. . . . But the vital question for a church is not so much whether it will continue to live, but whether it will remain that which it has been and which according to its innermost essence it ought to be.[18]

Orthodox Lutherans charge the Lutheran CG movement with disloyalty to the Lutheran Symbols while siding with other theological confessions. Sasse observed a trend toward not discussing theology from the Confessional point of view: "The Lutheran Confessions no longer play the role in the life and in the theological thinking of the Missouri Synod—in fact, of all of American Lutheranism by far—which they played during the nineteenth century."[19]

Sasse, who was an accomplished church historian and key player in the beginnings of the ecumenical movement, said that you can determine one's theological conviction in the Lutheran faith by observing where one "draws the limits of church and church fellowship."[20] He wrote in this regard: "Is it possible for a Lutheran to admit in earnest that a Baptist is a Bible believing man? Luther would not do it. Is it possible for a Bible believing person to deny that Holy Baptism is the washing of regeneration and that the bread which we bless in the Lord's Supper is the Body of Christ? What kind of faith in the Bible is it that can deny these things?"[21] Other Confessionalists, such as Marquart, ask the same things of Lutheran CG advocates: "Hunter also holds that 'church growth teaching causes a church to come alive.' So which is it then, church growth teaching or the means of grace? They are not the same."[22]

Any attempt to say that one is theology and the other practice is false. Marquart reacts in this way: "Genuine theology always embodies itself in practice, and authentic practice is steeped in theology. Theology without practice is empty, and practice without theology is blind. Each is bankrupt without the other. McGavran himself . . . says much the same thing from his point of view."[23]

DOES WITTENBERG NEED PASADENA'S REFORMATION?

Prominent Lutheran CG experts openly have fellowship with non-Lutheran groups, as demonstrated by this candid statement by Luecke:

> I offer as an example my relation to Fuller Theological Seminary in Pasadena, California. It is an interdenominational school with representation from some 70 different church-body heritages. I was one of the few Lutherans. Fuller has a carefully formulated Statement of Beliefs. In fact, as vice president I was charged with

assuring subscription on the part of staff and students. Were the statements exactly the way a confessional Lutheran would formulate them? Mostly, but not exactly. For instance, the statement affirmed the importance of word and sacrament ministry. But it did not go on to define baptism and Lord's Supper, let alone to profess Real Presence.[24]

It is not surprising that Luecke could easily subscribe to this statement, since he sees it as just part of the whole "style" debate. Meanwhile, "substance"—the fact that this interdenominational school teaches works-centered outreach—overrides any nebulous interpretation of the Sacraments. Luecke affirms this, saying: "Other Lutherans may disagree. I propose we are in the realm of differing style for expressing the same substance of confessional integrity."[25]

This shows clearly that the CG movement, even for Lutheran CG adherents, denies the importance of pure doctrine and focuses all on saving the lost. CG is so focused on increasing numerical growth that doctrine becomes secondary. In fact, if doctrine causes loss of market share (attendance, membership, etc.), then it is minimized as "style." As a case in point, note Luecke's representative attitude toward closed Communion: "In one heated conference the question arose: Is closed communion substance or style? I handled it poorly. Today I would say, yes. The theology is substance. The way it is practiced is style."[26] He declares that what he believes is substance, citing 1 Corinthians 11:27–29 and 5:11 for support: communicants should be baptized Christians who "should be able to spiritually examine themselves for sin and repentance, and they should recognize that they receive the true body and blood of Christ in the bread and wine they are receiving."[27] They should not be in open, public sin. The "changeable style," as Luecke phrases it, is how individual pastors and their congregations administer this "substance" of the Lord's Supper.

This relates to size of worship attendance and the logistics of knowing the confession of each individual who desires the Sacrament. Luecke concludes: "If the Lutheran conditions are stated, then the loving and pastoral application is to commune those who think they qualify."[28]

But these are not the Lutheran conditions—not as they have been believed, taught, and confessed since the beginning. A 1999 Synod Resolution, reaffirmed by the Praesidium, challenges Luecke's "substance" argument:

> We recognize the pastoral responsibility the church has not merely to accept minimalist concessions to ill-defined and un-examined confessions of the faith, but instead to lead people into the truth of the Scriptures, so that they may enjoy the fellowship of the church as it gathers at the altar to receive her Lord's body and blood in the Sacrament of the Altar.

A portion of the 1998 Resolution 3-05, "Reaffirming Closed Communion," addresses Luecke's conditions:

> This "Real Presence" is not simply a general presence of Christ in the Supper, but refers to the fact that Christ's true body and blood are truly present in the consecrated bread and wine and received in the mouths of the communicants (1 Corinthians 10:16). The presence of Christ's true body and blood does not depend on the faith of the recipient nor on the character of the one administering the Sacrament, but on the Word of Christ Himself.[29]

It goes on to affirm the historic Lutheran and catholic belief that

> a responsible Lutheran practice surrounding the Lord's Supper will take into account the fact that the Supper is also an expression of the oneness of the congregation in Christ and in His Gospel. "For as often as you eat this bread and drink the cup, you proclaim the Lord's death until He comes" (1 Corinthians 11:26 RSV). One who

eats and drinks at an altar confesses what is taught from that altar (1 Corinthians 10:21). Each communicant is called on to examine himself before God (1 Corinthians 11:28), to avoid creating divisions within the assembly (1 Corinthians 11:17ff).

It concludes with this salient point: "As part of this practice the pastor will seek to prevent a profession of confessional unity in the faith where there is, in fact, disunity and disagreement."

What CG activists such as Luecke and Hunter advocate is not this kind of fellowship and unity, but one that goes beyond Lutheran confession and practice. Their written claims convey this sharp contrast concerning fellowship with non-Lutherans. Hunter says, "Of course, we want doctrinal purity, and we desire to be confessionally strong. But our primary task is not to defend the truth, but to share it. That is the real war and the essential battle that is before us."[30] Luecke concurs: "The traditional LCMS approach views others as heterodox when they were not in agreement on all details of a church body's confession. That is a very narrow definition that may have fit the times of the nineteenth century. Does that traditional interpretation have to extend now to ministry in the twenty-first century?" Luecke wants to "reach out to fellow Christians as far as possible without compromising confessional integrity. . . . Somewhere between inside the small circle and outside the large circle are a great many Christians who offer opportunities for ministries that Lutheran congregations can learn from and support on the way to more effectively touching lives with the Gospel."[31]

Confessionalists cannot help but respond with amazement that CG advocates are more concerned with "effective outreach" than maintaining the pure Gospel. If one's primary theological concern is not the doctrine of justification, but rather the saving of some through any old generic gospel, then the result is a rapid, indiscriminate acceptance of heterodox confessions, coupled with attacks on those faithful to Lutheran beliefs and practices.[32]

A FINAL THOUGHT

An LCMS banquet speaker put it well: "If you woke many LCMS pastors from a dead sleep and asked: 'What kind of Christian do you really want to be?' they would answer: Baptist, Pentecostal, Evangelical—anything but Lutheran. Then they'd catch themselves and answer: 'Oh, I was asleep. I'm a confessional Lutheran.'"[33]

What is being touted as true Lutheranism in substance while using techniques from other sources as style is plain deception. Whether CG advocates are ready to admit it in public or not, they seem to have lost their first love. Perhaps they are ashamed of the Lutheran way. They should be more honest with themselves and their congregations and with the Synod if they do not believe in Lutheran theology as a viable confession of God's truth for the salvation of souls.

A wise Lutheran once told me, "You can judge a pastor's theology by observing his library and talking to him about what he has been studying." CG pastors are studying and learning from all kinds of talented people in many fields and theologies except those that are of a Lutheran nature. These they shy away from.

Just think: to place Donald McGavran in the same line with Martin Luther and the apostle Paul! Luther refused to shake Zwingli's hand at the Marburg Colloquy when Zwingli would not confess the true presence of Christ in the Sacrament. Paul refused fellowship with the apostles James, Peter, and John until he was certain that they all believed the same confession of the truth (Galatians 2:9). Isn't it amazing, then, that such a prominent CG expert as Hunter—who also confesses to be Lutheran—openly aligns with a foreign theology from Pasadena and promotes it as the cure for what is wrong with the LCMS? Jesus' statement that one cannot serve two masters at the same time applies to one's theological allegiance as well.

Truth be told, it is not only CG pastors who find more in common with the clergy of other confessional bodies. I myself often find more agreement with area clergy of the WELS church than I do with many of my own LCMS brethren. I am only too aware that the same is true for those of the CG persuasion—that they find far more agreement with mission-oriented clergy at parachurch gatherings such as Promise Keepers and John Maxwell seminars than they do with real Lutherans. This points up the rapidly growing dysfunctionality among us. We are not even close in most of our doctrinal beliefs and practices anymore. We find ourselves in a painful and tense situation. Lord have mercy!

9

CAN ANYTHING GOOD COME FROM PASADENA?

CHURCH GROWTH CLAIMS:

To be evangelical is not only to have a doctrinal position on the evangel, the good news, but also to have a priority to get the Word out. If evangelism is such a strong value, why shouldn't it be a priority for sharing with lost people? . . . There are those, too, who claim to be "confessional." Unfortunately, this has become an academic stand rather than a dynamic movement. Confessional activities are reduced to academic discussions, debates, and other presentations to Christians to help them make sure they believe the right things, in the right way. Confessions explain, enlighten, and help Christians to take a clear stand. There is nothing wrong with this activity, but if it ends at that, confessionalism becomes an academic exercise which misses the force of confessing the Gospel, which is proclaiming it to those who haven't yet heard it.[1]

CONFESSIONAL LUTHERAN CLAIMS:

Some emphases of the Church Growth Movement have highlighted the importance of mission work and a desire for healthy growth. There is certainly nothing wrong with common sense suggestions that might make a church more accessible and relational—the need for visibility, adequate parking space and facilities, ways of making a congregation more welcoming to new members, and the like. Such ideas can be helpful.[2]

Calling into question certain features of the Church Growth Movement should by no means lessen our churches' commitment to evangelize the lost.[3]

A terrible idea has been afoot in Christian circles for a long time. It has taken many different forms. If our Synod is to carry out its resolve to tell the good news about Jesus, we must face this idea head-on and correct it. The terrible idea is that doctrine and evangelism do not mix, that they are related to one another like water is related to fire. Perhaps you have heard it said, "Are we concerned about doctrine, or are we concerned about people?" Concern about doctrine has at times suffered in the name of evangelism. . . . Concern about doctrine was sacrificed to what people were convinced was the cause of evangelism. There is another side to this matter, exemplified today by pastors and others who spend so much time on the finer points of theology or at least on what they think is indispensable to such fine points that they take no opportunity to tell the good news about Jesus to the unchurched. They run out of time, for they allow themselves to run out.[4]

NOT EITHER/OR, BUT BOTH/AND!

Is there anything salvageable from the CG movement? Some will immediately answer no. However, this is not the position of many of the Confessional mind-set. Most will readily admit that the CG commitment to evangelize the lost is vital, and they are united with CG on this issue.

Sainted LCMS president A. L. Barry agreed with Lutheran CG advocates in the pressing need to "get the Good News out." He campaigned long and hard for "pulling out all the stops" to share Christ with a perishing world:

> It is impossible for us to come away with a smugly contented and self-satisfied attitude as regards the church and its role in the world. Acts tells us of a persistent, even pugnacious church that did not wait for the world to come to it. It went into the world with the gospel message, confronting unbelief and unbelievers with the sword of the Spirit, even in situations where everything seemed stacked against the evangelistic cause. Nor did the church wait until all its internal problems were solved before it reached out.[5]

The lack of doctrinal discernment with the Lutheran CG movement is troubling, but equally troubling is the lack of concern for evangelism that some Confessional pastors and congregations exhibit. Certainly Dr. Barry would not condone this, nor would many Confessional pastors. Doctrine and evangelism go together. They both are vital, necessary, and biblical. Continued admonition and encouragement should be given to both!

Pastors and congregations that have no desire for outreach and growth should be disciplined and given good pastoral counsel. The CG charges of academic interest at the expense of outreach are in some cases embarrassingly true. Taking an "either/or" stance toward doctrine and evangelism must be rejected by all, CG and Confessionalists alike.

It is vital that a truly Lutheran missiology, based on Scripture and the Confessions, be written, published, and implemented. The Confessionalists who served on the Church Growth Study Committee concur: "In addition to the responsibility of keeping safe every soul in the church for the Lord Jesus, the church also has the responsibility to conduct an effective soul-winning program."[6] This effort must receive our priority and resources. Pastors and congregational leaders are

> to bring their congregation's worship life and outreach into harmony with Scripture and our Lutheran Confessions. Then out of loyalty to Christ and our love for the lost, each congregation must explore new opportunities to tell the Good News, asking such questions as . . . How can we bring the secular world to the church without secularizing the church? . . . How can we strengthen our members as royal priests in their daily vocations, demonstrating Christian virtue in a culture growing increasingly godless and wicked? [7]

This report goes on to declare that there are many ways to obtain the attention of those now outside of God's mercy. The greatest thing we can do is "bring the greatest numbers possible into contact with God's Word and Sacraments." We are confident that "all those who hear and believe also will be gathered into Christ's church in earth and heaven. This is our conviction in the Lutheran Church—Missouri Synod. And so God's mission continues among us and through us: Tell the Good News about Jesus."[8]

OTHER BLESSINGS FROM CG

From CG comes much useful information. There is much we can agree with, from helps in the promotion of the church to common-sense concerns that our facilities and properties be attractive, safe, and inviting to our communities. An unchristian, unlutheran attitude of "take us as we are" or "we don't care if you come or not" is to be discouraged. Away with cold, unfriendly churches where visitors are not greeted warmly. In this we are united.

To be sure, we as LCMS members desire for Christ's

church to be successful, relevant, and influential in our culture and communities. We can and should utilize all available technologies and resources that aid us in this outreach to our world. Evangelism starts at home. We must fervently desire to be Christ's fishermen for men and women, young and old, of all races and classes. That means getting a line wet, not just sitting around talking about fishing.

We must admit that much of our growth in the glory days of the Synod resulted from internal birth rates as well as from the immigration of Lutherans from Europe and elsewhere to our nation. We were a very successful church, blessed by God's grace with His pure Gospel, gathering these people into fellowship around His Word and Sacraments. Now we look for God-pleasing opportunities to extend His kingdom by going out to those around us with our personal witness and with our congregational and synodical messages. "Tell the Good News about Jesus," a major thrust of our Synod in these early days of the twenty-first century, is evidence of our emphasis on witness. It must be a continuous priority. Naturally, God's chosen people are to be about seeking the lost and allowing God's power, His Gospel, to return these lost sheep back to His fold. Lutheran Hour Ministries has such a wonderful expression: "Bringing Christ to the Nations and the Nations to the Church."

Our stewardship of the mysteries of God is severely lacking if we do not devote the firstfruits of our finances, time, and talents to "getting this message out while keeping the message straight," as A. L. Barry put it. Some Confessionalist pastors and their congregations seem to equate intentional outreach with CG and therefore regard outreach as somehow tainted, unbiblical, and unlutheran. This needs to be corrected and monitored just as adamantly and fervently as our vigilance against false doctrine. We all sin at times by being ashamed of confessing Christ before our adulterous generation (Matthew

10:32–33; Mark 8:38) and of hiding the light before this sin-darkened world (Matthew 5:14–16). Confessionalists agree with Hunter in saying that the priesthood of all believers "is sent with those nonprofessional people into the business world, the schools, the stores, and the streets."[9] In another place Hunter says, "True evangelism might be well defined as a combination of beliefs and values. While many people may believe that a person without faith in Christ is without hope for eternal life and will be condemned to hell, they may not value the person without Christ sufficiently to suffer the discomfort of witnessing to him."[10]

To be faithful in keeping the doctrine pure while seeking opportunities to share Christ is merely to be a Christian. Dr. Barry declares: "Doctrine and evangelism are wedded in the history of the early church. This union lies embedded, for example, in the book of Acts. Let no one put asunder what God has joined together!"[11] He goes on to expose the common self-ishness that makes us so inwardly focused that we don't let in any "undesirables." Dr. Barry provides the scriptural corrective: "We believe that God loved the world, but we find it hard to think that he loved certain 'undesirables' and that He wants us to share our love with them as well as the blessings of salvation. We also need to get the message about mission to the Gentiles. It is a good thing this message is repeated so often in Acts."[12]

Dr. Barry has made it clear that Confessionalists in the Synod need not only to talk about outreach but to perform outreach with zeal. As he said at the Synodical Convention in 1998:

> It is the challenge to you, my brother pastors and other full time church workers, that we in our own personal lives witness to Jesus Christ to those with whom we come into contact, and that as we have never done so before. It is the challenge to you, our lay leadership and to the members of your congregations, that we vigorously tell the good news of Jesus in our various activities and call-

ings in life. It is the challenge to our seminary and our college professors that we weave into the fabric of all of that which they are teaching the goal of reaching people for Jesus Christ. It is the challenge to our Synod's boards and commissions, to our Districts and synodical leaders, that we keep this emphasis in mind as we plan and unfold all that we do so that we help our Synod to tell the good news about Jesus. It is a challenge to our congregations, Districts, yes, our Synod, to grab hold of this 3/10 Emphasis and with one unified voice say—"As we move into the final years of this present century, and the opening years of the next, we are going, with great zeal—with great zeal—to reach out to those around us who do not know Jesus Christ and the good news of His salvation. And we are going to do it with untiring vigor in the Lord."[13]

Every member of the Synod is reminded—as Dr. Barry liked to say in his speeches about his own personal challenges—to tell someone each day about the salvation given to us in Jesus Christ. He relates this to each of us:

I would also maintain that your own personal "To the Ends of the Earth" is as close as people with whom you daily come into contact, an arm's length away. It starts with your own family, husband, wife, children, grandchildren. Let me ask you—when was the last time that you spoke with your spouse, your children, your grandchildren, about your faith in Jesus Christ and the joy of that salvation that is yours? But it doesn't stop there. It also involves those people with whom we work, the neighbor across the street, the person with whom we have coffee, the family down the way, yes, and even those casual people with whom we daily come into contact along life's road.[14]

Both sides in this controversy declare that the Good News of salvation in Christ is uncontainable! Dr. Barry declares:

This is the thing about the gospel message that will not stay contained. Since salvation is full and free in Jesus

Christ, it is for everyone. Justification provides a basis for universal mission, evangelism to all people. It also constitutes the most powerful tool to be used in evangelism. The message of justification by grace reaches out to people right where they are, dead in trespasses and sins, without hope and without God in the world.[15]

Confessionalists thank God for this continued emphasis, which they, together with CG, can affirm and encourage.

ACADEMIA MUST SERVE THE CHURCH

The historic Christian church has moved through eras in which an educated clergy and academic institutions have come under attack. Sometimes this is warranted, while sometimes it must be challenged.

What is warranted is criticism aimed at an ecclesiastical academia that becomes unattached from and disinterested in the life of the church. Academia can at times simply live in the past, comfortable and protected from all contemporary movements. As Hunter illustrates:

> Confessional activities are reduced to academic discussions, debates, and other presentations to Christians to help them make sure they believe the right things, in the right way. Confessions explain, enlighten, and help Christians to take a clear stand. There is nothing wrong with this activity, but if it ends at that, confessionalism becomes an academic exercise which misses the force of confessing the Gospel, which is proclaiming it to those who haven't yet heard it.[16]

Confessionalists disagree with the direction Hunter and CG take in their critique of academia. Hunter argues that the CG movement is "in its very essence, the best of what it means to be evangelical and confessional! Church Growth advocates today are not introducing anything new to the church. We are making a major attempt to bring the church back to a confessional and evangelical posture once again. We are attempting to put the Gospel out front first, as a priority, where it belongs."[17] What is missing, he says, is seminary training in witnessing rather than interpreting and preaching the Bible. Confessionalists counter that witnessing is simple—know what the Bible says and then preach, teach, and witness.

What is at stake here is the curriculum for our seminaries. Hunter charges: "Unfortunately, most of the structures of the church are designed towards the means rather than the end. They are primarily confessional and only minutely confessing. They are, for the most part, geared toward doctrinal academics and only occasionally directed toward what it really means to be evangelical."[18] Marquart responds by challenging Hunter's basic assumption that we Lutherans have not been evangelistic dynamos because of some defect in our doctrine, our seminary training, or our outdated tradition. Marquart simply insists that we be motivated by the means of grace and evangelize as Lutherans.

What is being debated here is not outreach per se. To CG we say that a Lutheran should witness with a Lutheran confession of the faith. To Confessionalists we say that a Lutheran with a Lutheran confession of the faith should witness. Dr. Barry says, "So in our day, we can ask: in our various outreach efforts, are we remaining faithful to the great truth of justification by grace? It is too good to be true, but it is true! And are we standing on the Scriptures? There is no way we can consider the audience—not the message—to be sovereign."[19]

The CG critique of our seminaries and academia fails to acknowledge and appreciate that there are generalists and specialists in the church. As Dr. Barry tells us:

> I am reminded of one churchman who said it would be good for theologians to swap places with frontline missionaries for a while. But of course, pastors and laypeople in congregations cannot afford the luxury of overspe-

cialization. Those on the front lines have to be concerned about both faithfulness *and* outreach, doctrine *and* evangelism, confession of the truth *and* confessing the truth. Thanks be to our good and gracious God, this is exactly where the Scriptures equip us all to be.[20]

A FINAL THOUGHT

What is to be sovereign in the church of Christ—the audience or the message? Here we have come full circle. We began with a discussion about pleasing people or God. We have heard the CG focus on the unchurched. An excellent NT exegete, D. A. Carson, asks in his book *The Gagging of God*, "If Christianity is primarily a religion in which God exists to meet my needs, how can it be truly God-centered? How can we avoid the rising number of 'specialists' who cater to the rising number of confusing needs?"[21]

Gagging God? Both sides claim that this is done, either when one does not speak to the lost when given the opportunity or when one speaks false words to these unchurched persons. Lutherans are convinced that the Gospel of Jesus Christ must be preached to the entire world, and then the end may come (Matthew 24:14). In the common conviction of the need to witness to the world, there is no controversy. We join in praying for and fervently seeking ways to do such sharing in a winsome manner.

However, there is still disagreement over the content and purity of this witness. Confessionalists do not believe in the divorcing of substance and style. It betrays a false conviction in one's theology to say that the end is what is vital, not the means. Likewise, just as fatal and displeasing to God is to believe that the audience—the unchurched—should control these means. Luther himself would never have allowed any doctrinal compromise under the guise of "missions" to replace the one thing that will save a lost soul—justification by faith.

As Dr. Barry noted:

> Justification becomes the beating heart of all our doctrinal faithfulness to God, for it lies at the center of all our church's teaching. Luther, who knew a thing or two about this topic, said that justification by faith "is the chief point and cornerstone, which alone begets, nourishes, builds, preserves and defends the church of God; and without it, the church of God is not able to subsist for a single hour." Or, putting the same thing another way, he said, "Where this single article remains pure, Christendom will remain pure, in beautiful harmony, and without any schisms. But where it does not remain pure, it is impossible to repel any error and heretical spirit."

We in the LCMS must take all the "gags" off God. We must not gag Him by our arrogant contentment, ignoring those outside the faith with our "let them come if they want to be saved" attitude. Neither can we wait until all of our internal issues are reconciled before we can be such witnesses. We must be about our Father's business! Nor can we dare presume that we have pure confession and then apply foreign techniques and methodologies, thinking we are still serving the end goal while letting the yeast pour into the dough. Sheep without a faithful shepherd have a constant junk-food diet. Predatory wolves will be welcomed into the fold. We must not gag God with unbiblical "style."

A book about one of my hobbies is analogous to our Synod's current situation. *Soul of a Chef: The Journey towards Perfection* is about the individual styles and philosophies of three distinguished gourmet chefs: Brian Polcyn of the Five Lakes Grill in Milford, Michigan; Michael Symon of Lola Bistro in Cleveland; and Thomas Keller of Napa Valley's The French Laundry.[22] The first chef, Brian Polcyn, is obsessed with achieving the title "master chef." He has worked very hard to gain command of many culinary techniques—even ones that are really no longer in demand. Let this chef represent the pastors within our Synod who value very highly the skills of academia and tend toward repristination.[23] They do so at the cost of becoming isolated from the realities of the modern-day church and seem at times to be living in another era, totally isolated in their ivory towers and oblivious to what Christ and Antichrist alike are doing in God's vineyard.

The second chef, Michael Symon, has the opposite philosophy. He is aligned with the contemporary cultural scene. Although he has attended the best culinary schools, he disregards most of his schooling and has learned to provide what the pop-restaurant scene desires. He bends all the rules. He claims that he's merely sensitive to the current climate for food. Give the customers what they want! And he does, with such class and style that customers swoop in every night to his booming business. A true and classic "marketing" approach to fine food: supply the demand. Keep changing your menu, because what was hot last week and last month won't be tomorrow. Let this chef represent the CG segment of the LCMS.

The last of the three chefs, Thomas Keller, represents the best of each approach. He is formally trained and utilizes most of the classic, traditional techniques. And he is in demand! He does everything well. He draws people in. He is not content to just put out food; he puts it out with the best of preparation and presentation. He's mindful to keep everything orderly and clean, and demands pure tastes from the purest ingredients. Nothing is distorted or diluted. He doesn't especially desire the recognition he receives from the culinary world. His goal is to only put forward the very finest of food, and the quality generates the response. Let him represent the best of the Confessional pastors, concerned with giving to the sheep the very purest of Gospel and distributing the Sacraments as the Lord has directed. Growth and recognition are the Lord's doing. The Confessional pastor is not concerned with them. He is the Lord's man. He seeks to be pleasing to Him only.

10

MAINTAIN THIS WORK
OF CONCORD IN OUR LAND

CHURCH GROWTH CLAIMS:

Going arm-in-arm suggests uniformity. Journeys on the
same road suggest that the mission—getting to the right
destination—is the basis of unity. Focus on the common
mission allows for diversity in how the road is traveled.[1]

Implicit in this shift from national to local is acceptance
of greater diversity. A point of pride in the 1950s was that
you could go into any congregation of a church body like
the LCMS and they would be worshiping in the same
format with the same texts as any other congregation.
You could be spiritually at home wherever you were.
Now congregations, especially the growing ones, have
many styles of worship. It is the trend toward diversification that Lutherans in particular are having a hard time
accepting.[2]

Who is out of step? Going back to the University of Wittenberg, Lutheran heritage is oriented towards having
the pace set by faculty and their focus on truth. A reality
of church life in America today is the withering of

denominational influence; the vitality now rests with the local congregations, especially those that add effectiveness to concern about truth. It is inevitable that the growing churches will set the pace, unless they are forced out of the organization. In the Missouri Synod many of the largest have now established their own Pastoral Leadership Institute to better train ordained pastors to meet their needs.[3]

In spite of all the rhetoric of those who claim "confessional purity," the truth is that Church Growth represents the authentic, Reformation evangelical movement of focused Christianity.[4]

The question before every church today is whether it will be business as usual or whether the church will become a mission. The question before every Christian today is whether it will be business as usual or whether each of us will become missionaries. I predict that any local congregation which does not take on a mission posture within the next 10 years will be non-existent as a local church within 50 years. I also believe that any denomination that doesn't significantly take on a mission posture within the next 20 years will not exist as a viable denomination in 70 years. Of course, to perpetuate an institution is not the objective of the Christian movement anyway, but to lose the institution is a certain result of those churches which cling to the packaging of an age that no longer exists and barricade the Gospel within the walls of their own self-centeredness. The good news is that today thousands of churches are retooling, reprioritizing.[5]

CONFESSIONAL LUTHERAN CLAIMS:

When Herman Sasse tried to wake his slumbering fellow-Lutherans with the question about the very survival of the Lutheran church, he had in mind something else. What is the meaning of this question? For one thing, it cannot mean a glib recipe for success, like the popular sacrilege of "goal-setting," with the goal of Lutheran survival assured by keeping abreast of up-to-date trends with a Pandora's box full of clever methods and techniques. What will "survive" in this way may well call itself "Lutheran," but it will have nothing to do with the Lutheran confession, which on the contrary will be happily-clappily trampled underfoot to the soft seduction or the raucous savagery of "Christian music." Of course the "right doctrine and church" will survive—it is built on the Rock and cannot fail. The question is, will we? With us or without us, through us or despite us, God will see His "right doctrine and church" through. . . . What matters here is not our assessment of the future, but our faithfulness in the present. . . . Sasse called it "blasphemy" to expect the Holy Spirit to remove the obstacles which we ourselves willfully put in the way of His working. . . . Can the Lutheran confession be a mere "theological direction" or trend within a larger church, which as such gives equal rights to other confessions? Is our confession content to be a private interest or hobbyhorse within non-Lutheran churches, or does it define the boundaries of the orthodox church and demand that church-fellowship observe them?[6]

The Synod in convention wholeheartedly adopted the outreach emphasis of "Tell the Good News about Jesus." There could not be a better theme and motive for a church body that believes and practices that God causes His growth through the means that He has given us, the Word and Sacraments. These means do, in fact, bring people to faith, as they have for centuries. Dire warnings that churches will "die" unless new and questionable methods are employed cast doubt upon God's faithfulness and His active work in bringing sinners to Himself. We do not need anything new or unique to cause growth; God can and will grow His church by the means God has given the church.[7]

TENSION

The solutions are strikingly opposed. CG says change over to the CG paradigm or perish. Confessionalists declare that the church of Christ will survive by proclaiming the true Gospel without sociological, marketing, or management measures. The Gospel needs no supplements. It saves without any help from cultural trendiness. A. L. Barry maintains that catechesis is necessary for concord:

> Catechesis is much more than simply imparting facts about Christianity. Catechesis is the ongoing application of the Word of God to the lives of people so that there is a renewing of their minds and hearts in conformity with the will of Jesus Christ. . . . Perhaps we in the Lutheran church have grown too accustomed to thinking about catechesis only in terms of youth and adult confirmation. As a result, catechesis is viewed as a "program" which has a definite beginning, mid-point, and conclusion. . . . This lifetime of catechesis leads us into a deeper appreciation for the church's history, its doctrines, its practices and all that these mean for the Christian. Catechesis is critical to the church's ongoing life and health. To the extent that catechesis is neglected in our church, it will falter and stumble. Without good catechesis the church will no longer be able to understand the teachings of the faith, but will only be able to bear witness to vague impressions or the emotional feelings that "being in church" may produce. Without consistently faithful catechesis, the church will slowly forget its history, its teachers, its traditions, and its wonderful heritage of faith. Without sound catechesis, each generation of Christians will be led to think that they are the first ever to have come to a living relationship with the Lord, and thus will be cut off from the wisdom of the ages of men and women down through the years who have struggled in life and have remained faithful. Stated very simply, catechesis is the key to the church's health and survival.[8]

Like our Lord was prone to do, he uses an illustration from agriculture:

> I grew up in southwestern Iowa. If you have ever been through that part of the country, you will no doubt remember seeing miles and miles of cornfields, and you will remember that it can get pretty hilly. As a teenager I would occasionally go out and work on one of my uncles' farms. One of their big problems was erosion. At the beginning, an eroding ditch was not all that big a problem, but if left unattended, the ditch would grow wider and wider and still wider until the time came when my uncle would no longer be able to get across it with his wagon. I see this happening among us in regard to catechesis. We need to recognize the erosion that has taken place and take steps to make sure that it does not continue. We need to reclaim lost ground.[9]

CG responds that maturity in the Scriptures is required, but not by means of any doctrinal concentration. What is most important is equipping the ministers of God, the laypeople, with spiritual gifts and training to share their faith. Kent Hunter says:

> Discipleship training without on-the-job involvement is an academic exercise that creates very learned people who are apathetic evangelicals in the true sense of the word. The church becomes filled with those people who know the right things. They are right, dead right. This is not just an optional approach to Christianity. It is unbiblical and leads to the decline and death of the Christian church. While so-called evangelicals have been busy defending the truth as an end in itself, thousands of Christians have failed to recognize what it means to be the church. Many do not know what it means to be the church, because they don't have a clue what the primary purpose of the church is.[10]

It always comes back to where we began. This controversy is about the primary purpose of the church. CG says mission. Confessionalists say pure Gospel. All the rest—barriers to the Gospel, effectiveness or faithfulness, vision and leadership, pastors as divine gifts or everyone a minister—depends on one's paradigm. Which will it be: Lutheran pure and simple or Lutheran mixed with CG?

ENOUGH, ALREADY!

Kurt Marquart exclaims, "Enough! 'Church Growth' is a mission paradigm shaped by a type of theology which as a whole does not square with the Lutheran understanding of the Gospel."[11] CG does not believe or practice that the Gospel purely preached and purely administered in the Sacraments is able to save anyone anymore! It needs to be modernized, not just for the culture, but also specifically for the culture in one particular area, i.e., the congregational setting.

The two camps are already far apart and are moving farther apart, and they both realize this. There does not seem to be any middle ground. CG's continual request, if not demand, is that diversity be tolerated in our Synod. David Luecke claims that our Synod is more like the Southern Baptist Convention: whatever the congregations in convention agree to is binding only "so far as the member congregations allow them to be."[12] According to Luecke, our being about the same mission journey—the right destination—is the basis for unity. He says, "Focus on the common mission allows for diversity in how the road is traveled."[13] To do this, we need as a Synod to organize ourselves more around mission diversity to achieve the objectives of outreach and get all to adapt to this movement. Luecke states: "To remain effective today, church bodies will need to recognize and support greater diversity among their congregations and thereby also learn to function with a greater decentralization of authority."[14]

Confessionalists counter that this diversity may be acceptable to other Christian church bodies, but not to Lutherans. Marquart claims: "It cannot recognize anything other than the purely preached Gospel and the rightly administered sacraments as constituting 'the right doctrine and church,' and therefore the boundaries of church fellowship (Augsburg Confession VIII, and Formula of Concord, S.D. X, 31)."[15] This confession sets the boundaries for fellowship and leaves no such room for "diversity" just to reach a mission-paradigm vision. Marquart claims that this non-Lutheran preoccupation with diversity came to the surface during the so-called "Statement of the 44" in 1945:

> Here the whole traditional understanding of the church and church fellowship was scuttled. Before, the objects of fellowship were churches, and the criteria were the objective marks of the church, the purely preached Gospel and the rightly administered sacraments. Now the whole notion of Orthodox Church and confession was dissolved into a sentimental pre-occupation with footloose individuals—so-called "other Christians." The old talk about confessions and confessional differences was replaced with talk about "denominations" and "denominational differences." Confession had dealt with truth, doctrine, and theology. "Denomination" suggested mere sociological description.[16]

He goes on to show how this has been manifested through fellowship with such parachurch, interdenominational movements as the Evangelical Alliance of 1846 and the current Promise Keepers. However, he claims that the "most devastating effect of the collapse of the confessional understanding of the church was the development of an unlutheran, but bureaucratically entrenched missiology, which thought it could stitch together an 'effective' strategy from bits of McGavran, C. Peter Wagner, Lyle Shaller, Carl George, and the like. When one criticizes this shapeless amalgam one is told that one is opposed to missions."[17]

To affirm pure confession is not to oppose missions. One cannot have a one-way street. Confessionalists like Marquart believe the Lutheran faith *is* mission, that it is ecumenically minded in the proper way while maintaining purity of doctrine: "The real missionary magnetism of the Book of Concord, and its remarkable power over the minds and souls of people, lie not in any clever packaging (would that we could do it better!), but in the attraction of that uncorrupted Gospel of Life itself which is there faithfully confessed."[18]

Marquart goes on to ask: what other confession teaches all that the Lutheran confession does? He responds:

> Certainly not Geneva, despite its laudable zeal for the Bible. Eastern Orthodoxy comes closest in its liturgical links with Christian antiquity, but its conventional theology is marred by synergism and moralism, not to mention the para-Christian cults of departed saints and the Blessed Virgin. The Roman liturgy, too, retains ancient treasures, but is sadly flawed by the sacrificial conception of the mass. Official Roman dogma cruelly distorts and disfigures the Mystery of Salvation. The Lutheran confession exalts this Mystery as does no other, but Lutheran church life has rarely lived up to its official confession—and therein lies the great tragedy of our church.[19]

OFFERS OF ALTERNATIVE SOLUTIONS?

Thus we are brought to this question: what shall the Synod do to get back on the right path?

CG answers: respect the diversity that has arisen among us. Everyone must embrace the CG mission paradigm or they will cease to exist. Change with the times or go under. Unless the people see with "CG eyes," they will perish. We cannot go back to the old LCMS ways of pure doctrine. That will not bring growth anymore. As one CG advocate contends, the trend of holding worship that caters to the unchurched and raising up laypeople with spiritual gifts to do the official ministry "at this point can't be stopped, even if we wanted to."[20]

Confessionalists respond that the Synod must not just hope and pray that God will remove the obstacles to concord. We must remove the false teaching that is infecting the rest of God's people and creating schism and dissension among us. Marquart quotes from Sasse:

> We have confidence in the Lord of the church that He, Who raises the dead, can raise also dying and dead churches, just as He has also raised our heart, dead in sin, to faith. But we declare it to be superstition when people fancy that God would do by a miracle that which He has commanded us servants of the church [to do], and which we ever and again fail to do, from laziness and cowardice, from convenience and fear of men. He has commanded the servants of the Word, the shepherds of His flock, for the sake of the eternal truth and for the sake of the souls entrusted to them, to bear witness against false doctrine and to exclude it from the church. We declare it to be blasphemy, when people expect that the Holy Spirit will surely remove the obstacles, which we willfully put in the way of His working. We know that no confession ensures the purity of doctrine—what errors have penetrated the churches which actually preserved the Nicene and Chalcedonian Creeds, like the churches of the East and Roman Catholicism—but we also know that the doctrine of the church must suffer total ruin, and the Gospel die, where the confession of the truth is forgotten.[21]

A FINAL THOUGHT

As a former marketing executive, I have always marveled at the diversification strategy of General Motors (subsequently modeled in lesser forms at Ford and the former Dodge-Chrysler), one of the world's largest corporations. In essence their strategy to compete has been to offer many automobile companies as one company. If you don't like Chevrolet, then there's Buick. If you don't particularly like Buick, then there's Pontiac.

Infatuated with their discovery of what has been working in corporate America, LCMS CG practitioners have applied this to the church. If you don't like the historical Christian faith as handed down through the Confessional Lutheran church, then try a Lutheran version of charismatic worship. If our Lutheran/Pentecostal worship doesn't turn you on, then try our laid-back, down-home service with revival-time accents and a minimalist theology. Just give me that old rugged cross!

Not content with being "alternative," they then attack anyone who challenges them as one who doesn't have any heart for missions. This is false. If it were true, then the greatest missionary who ever lived, Paul of Tarsus, had no heart for missions. If there was ever a pastor who was serious about pure doctrine (keeping the message straight) and missions (getting the message out), it was Paul.

Let's not deceive ourselves anymore. Confessionalists show that CG tries to supplement the Gospel with technique. CG contends that if Confessionalists don't change to the mission paradigm, they will cease to exist. Some suggest that catechesis and dialogue are the answer. We've been doing that for decades now. It hasn't brought us any closer to concord. In fact, some declare we are farther apart now than before. We have heard each other's arguments too many times, reorganized, reshuffled, restated.

It is all about the precious, pure Gospel. Every Christian knows this. But we must not be naïve. Not every Christian body holds to the same confession of the Gospel. Since all other teachings of the church flow from this precious center, its purity or corruption affects all other doctrines. From adiaphora to worship to the Office of the Public Ministry to fellowship—these issues are all influenced by our understanding of the Gospel.

It's time. It's time to confess what we truly believe, teach, confess, and practice in our congregations. It's time to state where our loyalties truly are. How can one who claims to be a "Confessional Lutheran," one who has studied the Book of Concord and vowed to practice his ministry in conformity to this confession, also state:

> The church has become a relic. This is not the fault of the Gospel—which is relevant to all people at all times in every age and in every culture. It is because of our selfish, myoptic Nehushtanism. We have not only failed as the people of God, to be focused on the mission of the church, but we have miserably failed to be flexible in the forms and nonessentials that are cultural trappings of a delivery system of the unchanging Gospel. We have betrayed the Gospel, undermined the essence of the incarnation, and abandoned the powerful dynamic of our Reformation heritage. The Church Growth Movement is a call to return to our roots. It is a challenge to think like a missionary, act like an ambassador, and operate like a mission. The Church Growth Movement is a challenge to face a world that is in constant change—a world that demands dynamic strategies to get the unchanging Gospel delivered. In spite of all the rhetoric of those who claim "confessional purity," the truth is that Church Growth represents the authentic, Reformation evangelical movement of focused Christianity.[22]

It's time for each man to state before God and His church his allegiance. I believe that the warning Jesus gave each of us, that one cannot serve two masters at the same time (Matthew 6:24), applies here: one cannot serve both CG and Christ! You will either love CG and all it stands for and serve that paradigm, or you will love being the "bond-slave" of the pure

Gospel of Jesus Christ and suffer all, even a declining membership and charges of cultural irrelevancy from the unchurched, rather than allow one ounce of false doctrine to intrude. We need to move to such a commitment as pastors and as congregations in our beloved LCMS.

How to proceed? I offer the process used by our Confessional forefathers in the controversy following Luther's death in the mid-sixteenth century. The church was thrown into confusion over just what it meant to be a Lutheran and whether the Lutheran church should continue under that name and confession. Under the leadership of Martin Chemnitz, a group of theologians wrote and edited what became the Formula of Concord. Writing on the occasion of the Formula's 400-year anniversary, Robert Preus and Wilbert Rosin noted:

> That more than 8,000 theologians could agree on a statement of Christian doctrine after decades of discord and debate was indeed a significant achievement. That the Formula of Concord of 1577 has survived the test of 400 years is more significant. . . . The Formula is sufficient evidence of the enduring vitality and vigor of Lutheranism after the death of the Great Reformer. . . . Lutherans who seek peace and concord in the church today, not only among Lutherans, but among all Christians, can learn from the sixteenth-century experience. The renewed interest in the Formula of Concord at this time is not an interest growing merely out of the 400th anniversary. It is based on the firm conviction that a faithful study of the Holy Scriptures will lead to harmony and understanding, though not necessarily to external unity of all church organizations.[23]

We need the Lord to have mercy upon our poor Synod and send us a group of confessors today to help us find the same process that our fathers used in the sixteenth century:[24]

- **Step One: Establish and work from a corpus doctrinae.** Public doctrinal statements to which the church subscribes will be the only documents that may be quoted to defend one's position in theological controversy. For our fellowship, the Scriptures and the Book of Concord. No McGavran, Hunter, Pieper, or Marquart allowed.

- **Step Two: Define terms.** Carefully explain the meaning of critical terms, issues, and words so that everyone is speaking about the same thing. Chemnitz believed the majority of effort initially should be spent on this point. Clearly state the theological issue(s) under contention, e.g., One party believes the means of grace, God's Word and Sacraments purely preached and administered, is able to grow the church, while the other party contends that supplemental, stylistic aids must be added constantly to grow the church in our given culture of rapid change and animosity toward the church as a relic.

- **Step Three: Practice the art of precise talking.** Resist all naming of names, speaking of personalities, and misinterpreting of others' words. Always address the issues involved. Clarity and precision of speech prescribe more intense listening and less emotional speaking (James 1:19–20).

- **Step Four: Refer all points back to the Scriptures.** Use the original languages. Cite the church fathers where pertinent, as Chemnitz did.

- **Step Five: Be willing to say we don't know.** Leave some questions to the heavenly academy. We don't have all the answers to how, where, and why the church grows the way it does (John 3:8).

- **Step Six: Conclude with a formal written agreement for those in concord.** Those who refuse to sign are in discord.

Time must be allowed to have this document of concord drawn up. Wise men must be chosen to compose these representations of the issues under controversy and to clearly state the biblical, Confessional position. It's time to separate those who choose "pleasing people" and those who are "bond-slave servants" to Christ and His pure Gospel.

It's time! Too much is at stake: the Gospel and the salvation of souls. We cannot sit idly by, hoping and praying that this CG leaven will fade or that its followers will have a "Damascus-road experience" and be led back into the Confessional fold. We must hammer out concord through the same means used by our Confessional forefathers. Prophetic in foreseeing our very situation, they stated their intent in these final words before their signatures of concord:

> Likewise, we desire furthermore to agree in a friendly way among ourselves earnestly, using whatever means possible, to maintain this work of concord in our lands, according to our own and each community's circumstances, through diligent visitation in the churches and schools, through supervision of the presses, and through other salutary means. And should the present controversies about our Christian religion again surface or new ones arise, we agree that to protect against all kinds of scandal they be settled and reconciled in a timely way before given a chance to spread. (Preface to the Book of Concord, 24)

The new controversy of Church Growth has been allowed to spread for more than two decades among our Confessional churches, bringing a scandal from outside our confession. This scandal must be addressed now before it is given more time to spread. It's time for concord. It's time to show our allegiance. It's time to be Lutherans.

NOTES

INTRODUCTION

[1] E. Jerome McCarthy, *Basic Marketing: A Managerial Approach* (Homewood, Ill.: Richard D. Irwin, Inc., 1968), 9.

[2] Ibid., 11.

[3] I am indebted here to Jerry Schoenle of Ford Motor Corporation's Brand Management Department for suggesting David A. Aaker's books as references for this area: *Building Strong Brands* (New York: Free Press, 1996); *Brand Leadership* (New York: Free Press, 2000); and *Managing Brand Equity* (New York: Free Press, 1991). Jerry also graciously read the section on marketing and provided valuable feedback.

[4] Aaker, *Building Strong Brands*, 7–25.

[5] Ibid., 2–7 and 37–66.

CHAPTER 1

[1] Kent R. Hunter, *Confessions of a Church Growth Enthusiast* (Corunna, Ind.: Church Growth Center, 1997), 240.

[2] Church Growth Study Committee—LCMS, *For the Sake of Christ's Commission* (Jan. 2001), 7.

[3] See Herman Sasse's excellent treatments "The Future Reunited Church" and "The Ancient Undivided Church," *The Springfielder* (Summer 1963), 8ff. His conclusions are well documented, for example: "That the 'ancient undivided church' is a theological fiction becomes fully evident if we turn from the 'heresies' to the great 'schisms' of ancient Christendom" (16). "'By schisms rent asunder, by heresies distressed': This has been the situation of Christendom at all times. There has never been a visible ancient undivided church" (18). Interesting reading in this article is relevant to the current ecumenical efforts by Rome for a "Jubilee" reunion of the church propelled by the Y2K fervor (cf. 19–21; see also Commission on Theology and Church Relations—LCMS, *The Joint Declaration on the Doctrine of Justification in Confessional Lutheran Perspective* [1999]). On the myth still being spread that such a "golden age of Christian unity" occurred in the early beginnings of the United States, see the fine work by Mark A. Noll and John D. Woodbridge, *The Gospel in America* (Grand Rapids, Mich.: Zondervan, 1979). They comment in their analysis of

Christianity in America's infancy: "The danger . . . was that embattled Christians unwittingly began to shade the history of America, not so much by outright distortion but by a process of selecting only those items that preserved the myth that at one time America had been an harmonious Christian commonwealth. In its worst form, this sense of the past became more myth than history and allowed Christians to find shelter from the difficulties of their own day by retreating to a Christian America that never existed at all" (220) (used by permission).

[4] See two of the prominent LCMS CG advocates, Hunter, *Confessions,* 25–38; and David S. Luecke, *Apostolic Style and Lutheran Substance* (Lima, Ohio: Fairway, 1999), 7–8. To pursue the formation of the CG movement, see Donald A. McGavran, *Understanding Church Growth* (Grand Rapids, Mich.: Eerdmans, 1980).

[5] For a background view, see Hunter, *Confessions,* 25, 34–35; Commission on Theology and Church Relations—LCMS, "Evangelism and Church Growth: with Special Reference to the Church Growth Movement" (1987), 6a; and Luecke, *Apostolic Style,* 22–24.

[6] Hunter, *Confessions,* 31.

[7] My research was unable to determine who first originated this phrase as applicable to the LCMS. Billy Graham is widely believed to have made this evaluation, but I was unable to confirm or deny this.

[8] Jack T. Robinson, "The Spirit of Triumphalism in the LCMS: The Role of the 'A Statement' of 1945 in the Missouri Synod" (Ph.D. diss., Vanderbilt University, 1972).

[9] See the excellent work by Kurt Marquart, "'Church Growth' as Mission Paradigm: A Confessional Lutheran Assessment," in *Church and Ministry Today: Three Confessional Lutheran Essays* (Northville, S.Dak.: The Luther Academy, 2001), 51–146.

[10] Ibid., 53.

[11] For the layperson who is not familiar with these paradigms and their theological descendants, see Thomas Manteufel, *Churches in America* (St. Louis: Concordia Publishing House, 1994), 13–14.

[12] For example, see the famous Lutheran commentator R. C. H. Lenski, *The Interpretation of St. Paul's First and Second Epistles to the Corinthians* (Minneapolis: Augsburg, 1963); and the Pentecostal New Testament scholar Gordon D. Fee, *The First Epistle to the Corinthians* (Grand Rapids, Mich.: Eerdmans, 1987).

[13] Commission on Theology and Church Relations, "Evangelism and Church Growth," 51.

[14] For example, see George Barna, *Marketing the Church: What They Never*

Taught You about Church Growth (Colorado Springs: Navpress, 1988), 33.

[15] Martin Franzmann and Walter Roehrs, *Concordia Self-Study Commentary* (St. Louis: Concordia Publishing House, 1979), 176.

[16] George G. Hunter III, *Church for the Unchurched* (Nashville: Abingdon, 1996), 28–34 (used by permission).

[17] Ibid., 14.

[18] Walter A. Elwell, ed., *Evangelical Dictionary of Theology* (Grand Rapids, Mich.: Baker, 1984), 233.

[19] See especially J. Louis Martyn, *Galatians,* Anchor Bible (New York: Doubleday, 1997), 137–140.

CHAPTER 2

[1] Luecke, *Apostolic Style*, 52.

[2] Marquart, "'CG' as Mission Paradigm," 86.

[3] Luecke, *Apostolic Style*, 22ff.

[4] AC, VII, 1.

[5] George Barna, *Church Marketing: Breaking Ground for the Harvest* (Ventura, Calif.: Gospel Light/Regal Books, 1992), 28–29 (used by permission).

[6] Barna, *Marketing the Church*, 33.

[7] Roland Allen, *Missionary Methods: St. Paul's or Ours?* (Grand Rapids, Mich.: Eerdmans, 1962), 70.

[8] Ibid., 64.

[9] As a starting introduction to the views on this topic, see Luecke, *Apostolic Style,* 33–34; and Marquart, "'CG' as Mission Paradigm," 59–71. For a fuller treatment, see David F. Wells, *No Place for Truth or Whatever Happened to Evangelical Theology* (Grand Rapids, Mich.: Eerdmans, 1993); and Alister McGrath, *Evangelicalism and the Future of Christianity* (Downers Grove, Ill.: InterVarsity, 1995).

[10] Ed Lehman, *Canadian Lutheran* (Sept. 1991), cover.

[11] Hunter, *Confessions*, 177ff.

[12] Kurt Marquart, "The Church and Her Fellowship, Ministry and Governance," *Confessional Lutheran Dogmatics,* vol. 9 (Ft. Wayne, Ind.: International Foundation for Lutheran Confessional Research, 1990), 214.

CHAPTER 3

[1] Luecke, *Apostolic Style,* 49.

[2] Hunter, *Confessions*, 246–47.

[3] Ibid., 241.

[4] Marquart, "'CG' as Mission Paradigm," 126.

[5] Church Growth Study Committee, *Christ's Commission*, 5

[6] Hunter, *Confessions*, 29.

[7] This required change is especially related to the laypeople's enthusiasm to witness, evangelize, and assume more participative roles in the church. For example, Hunter states: "The New Testament church cared about the integrity of these means of grace. But they were not obsessed with its purity to the degree that they barred imperfect newcomers and robbed the church of its multiplicative power. They sought to take the Word into the marketplace and be the sent-out group of people that God intended .... There is no evidence that Jesus perceives His followers as gathering in an institutional form to become a sort of ecclesiastical museum where visitors come to peek at the means of grace and get blessed by the professional keepers of forgiveness. The church is only gathered to be scattered" (*Confessions*, 173). See also Luecke, *Apostolic Style*, 19–24.

[8] Paul T. Heinecke, Kent R. Hunter, and David S. Luecke, *Courageous Churches: Refusing Decline, Inviting Growth* (St. Louis: Concordia Publishing House, 1991): "The courage I read about is more than a synonym for some hard-to-define characteristic of authentic Christian congregational living. It is a distinct and precise first element in a sequence of serving that starts with courage, moves on to effectiveness, and concludes with success" (9).

[9] Ibid., 12.

[10] David S. Luecke, *The Other Story of Lutherans at Worship* (Tempe, Ariz.: Fellowship Ministries, 1995), 2.

[11] Ibid., 123.

[12] See Marquart, "'CG' as Mission Paradigm," 113–33.

[13] Luecke, *Apostolic Style*, 27.

[14] Ibid., 56–57.

[15] Gregory J. Lockwood, *1 Corinthians: Concordia Commentary: A Theological Exposition of Sacred Scripture* (St. Louis: Concordia Publishing House, 2000), 313, n. 17. See also the cassette recording of the radio discussion on this text on the program "Issues, Etc." with Rev. Todd Wilken and Dr. Lockwood. It may be obtained from Issues, Etc. at 800-844-0524. Ask for tape 3–13–00C. Of significance here also is the commentary on this passage from Gordon Fee: "This passage has often been looked to for the idea of 'accommodation' in evangelism, that is, of adapting the message to the language and perspective of the recipients. Unfortunately, despite the need for that discussion to be carried on, this passage does not speak

directly to it. This has to do with how one lives or behaves among those whom one wishes to evangelize" (*The First Epistle to the Corinthians*, 432). For an interesting view of accommodation or contextualization, see Kurt Marquart's article "Law/Gospel and 'Church Growth,'" in *The Beauty and the Bands: Papers Presented at the Congress on the Lutheran Confessions* (Crestwood, Mo.: Association of Confessional Lutherans, 1995), 184ff. He concludes: "Contextualization is a conceptual predator, and cannot with a few sentences be tamed into a safe house pet, to be left without further ado in charge of the whole farm!"

[16] Lockwood, *1 Corinthians*, 314.

[17] Ibid., 314.

[18] Hunter, *Confessions*, 240.

[19] Ibid., 240.

[20] Ibid., 244.

[21] Ibid., 136.

[22] Ibid., 138–39.

[23] See the excellent discussion of this issue in the report of the Church Growth Study Committee, *Christ's Commission*, 4–7.

[24] One can see this throughout the Confessions, e.g., AC, XXVI, 40; Ep. X, 4-5-2; SD, X, 9.30.

[25] Marquart, "'CG' as Mission Paradigm," 118.

[26] Matthew C. Harrison, "Martin Chemnitz and FC X," in *Mysteria Dei: Essays in Honor of Kurt Marquart* (Ft. Wayne, Ind.: Concordia Seminary Press: 1999), 79–99.

[27] Ibid., 92–93.

[28] Robert Kolb and Timothy Wengert, eds., *The Book of Concord* (Minneapolis: Augsburg Fortress, 2000), SD, X, 10.

[29] Marquart, "'CG' as Mission Paradigm," 52–64.

[30] Ibid., 54.

[31] See Church Growth Study Committee, *Christ's Commission*, 4–7.

[32] A. L. Barry, *The Unchanging Feast: The Nature and Basis of Lutheran Worship* (St. Louis: Office of the President, LCMS: 1995), 42.

[33] Hunter, *Confessions*, 237. He goes on: "There are varieties of Christians. We don't all agree on everything, and we never will, this side of eternity. The litmus test of whether a person is a Christian or not may be related to a question like this: 'Do you believe that that person with that different point of view, with that different doctrine, with that different emphasis, with that different style of worship, will go to heaven?' This is very reveal-

ing as to what the fire is behind all the smoke. Pure doctrine and unity in it is not that important. No one can have all the truth. Thus, unless you can say that a person does not have the minimum to go to heaven, then that person is an unchurched prospect for you to convert. LCMS has always confessed they have the truth, and all of it. We are not apologetic or ashamed that God has given us this gift of unity in the apostolic, catholic faith. As Francis Pieper puts it so well, 'The Fathers of the Missouri Synod declare it a calumny when the Lutheran Church is accused of identifying the Church of God with the Lutheran Church. They taught: If a person sincerely clings to the cardinal doctrine of the Christian faith, if he believes that God is gracious to him because of Christ's *satisfactio vicaria*, he is a member of the Christian Church, no matter in which ecclesiastical camp he may be.' . . . It is common knowledge that the presence of children of God in heterodox churches is urged to prove that it is right, even demanded by charity, to fellowship heterodox churches. This is the exact opposite of what Scripture teaches, for Scripture says, 'Avoid them.'"

CHAPTER 4

[1] Hunter, *Confessions*, 137.

[2] Luecke, *Apostolic Style*, 9.

[3] Robert W. Schaiblcy, "Lutheran Preaching: Proclamation, Not Communication," *Concordia Journal* 18 (Jan. 1992), 12–13.

[4] Church Growth Study Committee, *Christ's Commission*, 6.

[5] Barry, *The Unchanging Feast*, 46.

[6] Donald G. Matzat, ed., "Hitting for the Cycle," *Issues, Etc. Journal*, vol. 3, no. 2, (Spring 1998), 12–13.

[7] Luecke, *Apostolic Style*, 8.

[8] Ibid., 9. See also Hunter, *Confessions*, 137.

[9] See Alan C. Klaas, *In Search of the Unchurched* (New York: Alban Institute, 1996), 50–56. Also refer back to chapter 3 and the barriers discussed there and documented in the endnotes.

[10] See the frank facts laid out in CG expert consultant Lyle Schaller's book *The New Reformation: Tomorrow Arrived Yesterday* (Nashville: Abingdon, 1995), especially 69–79.

[11] Luecke, *Apostolic Style*, 9. Edwin L. Lueker, ed., *The Lutheran Cyclopedia: A Concise In-Home Reference for the Christian Family* (St. Louis: Concordia Publishing House, 1975), defines sacramentalism as "(1) View and practice that assigns to sacraments a higher inherent saving power than

the Word. (2) Belief that sacraments are inherently efficacious and necessary to salvation and can bestow grace on the soul. (3) Belief that nature and life have spiritual meaning and are symbols of the divine" (691).

[12] Luecke, *Apostolic Style*, 9.

[13] Hunter, *Confessions*: "Likewise, it is more important for a pastor to train other Christians to provide Christian counseling to those in need than to counsel those in need" (204).

[14] You will derive blessings from reading C. F. W. Walther, *The Proper Distinction between Law and Gospel*, trans. William H. T. Dau (St. Louis: Concordia Publishing House, 1928).

[15] Wilhelm Petersen, "Effective Law and Gospel Preaching," in *The Beauty and the Bands*, 105.

[16] Schaibley, "Lutheran Preaching," 13.

[17] Ibid., 13.

[18] Ibid., 16–20.

[19] Ibid., 16–17.

[20] Luecke, *Apostolic Style*: "The Promise Keepers movement is a good illustration. These conferences and follow-up small groups have had a strong Gospel impact on the lives of millions of men and families. God has richly blessed this innovative coalition of Evangelical leaders. Attitudes toward Promise Keepers can serve to differentiate Lutheran pastors and their mission orientation in some productive ways. Spot a Lutheran congregation that is openly supportive of Promise Keepers, and you probably have a Lutheran pastor more mission-minded than most of his colleagues. That congregation is also likely to worship differently from most others. I find nothing in the Promise Keepers' statement of faith that contradicts a Lutheran confession" (36).

[21] Al Janssen and Larry K. Weeden, eds., *Seven Promises of a Promise Keeper* (Colorado Springs: Focus on the Family, 1994), 8.

[22] Schaibley, "Lutheran Preaching," 23.

[23] As quoted in Fred L. Precht, ed., *Lutheran Worship: History and Practice* (St. Louis: Concordia Publishing House, 1993), 206.

[24] Ibid.

CHAPTER 5

[1] Interview: "Dr. Kent Hunter on Church Growth," *Concordia Student Journal*, vol. 9, no. 1 (1985), 11.

[2] Luecke, *Apostolic Style*, 123.

[3] Walter P. Kallestad, *Total Quality Ministry* (Minneapolis: Augsburg, 1994), 9–10.

[4] Church Growth Study Committee, *Christ's Commission*, 4.

[5] Klemet Preus, "Review of *Confessions of a Church Growth Enthusiast*, by Kent R. Hunter," *LOGIA X* (Epiphany 2001), 49.

[6] David K. Weber, "Account-ability," *Concordia Theological Quarterly* 65 (Jan. 2001), 47–48.

[7] Again, refer to Kent Hunter's interesting statement in on page 49, n. 7. Notice here Hunter's notion of the role of faithfulness to all of God's Word. Charity enters in while doctrine is not of any real import, even where the precious means of grace are concerned. Compare to Kurt Marquart's confession in "'CG' as Mission Paradigm." He states: "Still, when allowance has been made for organizational and other trivial differences, there remain the basic confessional divisions. These basic differences over doctrine are irreducible in that they express fundamentally different understandings of the Gospel itself. Are we saved by Christ's merit alone, or partly also by our own? . . . No honest Gospel proclamation can evade these specifics. There is no 'generic' Gospel which can somehow by-pass them, or form a common core beneath the contradictions. A 'Gospel' which deliberately fudges, evades, or waffles about them is not the Gospel in the sense of the New Testament (Galatians 1)!" (115–17).

[8] *Jesus First* 9 (June 2000), cover.

[9] Hunter, *Confessions*, 133. Interesting here is that this quote is in response to those who say the church will grow if the Word of God is preached and the Sacraments administered (which Hunter calls a "cop-out").

[10] Luecke, *Apostolic Style*, 25.

[11] While sometimes one of the main presenters, Hunter is featured in a recent brochure promoting a 2001 conference on "The Culture-Friendly Church: A Daring Approach to 21st Century Mission" as a special "added value"—"Dr. Kent Hunter, a widely respected church consultant heard nationally on the radio as 'The Church Doctor,' will provide individuals or groups with an opportunity to meet with him."

[12] Kallestad, *Total Quality Ministry*, 10.

[13] Hunter, *Confessions*, 159.

[14] Ibid., 160.

[15] Ibid., 161.

[16] Church Growth Study Committee, *Christ's Commission*, 2.

[17] Ibid., 6: "The key to how well the church thrives in today's culture is surely how well and how thoroughly the church teaches. This is not a

time to cut back church membership classes to one Saturday afternoon, as some are doing. This is not a time to turn Bible classes and the Sunday school into 'sharing times,' rather than training in God's Word. This is not a time to minimize doctrine, morality and discernment of error. Rather, the church must pay new attention to catechesis, not only of young people and new members but of the whole congregation struggling to live as Christians in a non-Christian culture."

[18] Heinecke, et al., *Courageous Churches.*

[19] Notice the contrast with the position of Art Just, "Luke 9:51–24:53" *Concordia Commentary* (St. Louis: Concordia Publishing House, 1997), 674–76.

[20] David P. Scaer, *The Sermon on the Mount* (St. Louis: Concordia Publishing House, 2000), 248–49. Very relevant here is the way the biblical text describes this tribulation and its connection with false prophets. Scaer comments: "The false prophets came disguised as legitimate bearers of the message of Jesus. Such a description does not seem to fit Jesus' contemporaries, who clearly identified themselves as his adversaries. The warning against the false prophets is basically an anticipatory and eschatological word of Jesus projected into the community of his followers. . . . This warning necessarily presupposes that he will no longer be there and a church structure will develop where many church leaders are making a claim on the allegiance of the people" (251). Scaer goes on to discuss the disclosure of these false prophets by their fruits in Matthew: "The Baptist asks the Pharisees and Sadducees to produce fruits that show they have repented, that they have accepted the coming of the Kingdom. John tells us no more than that they were confessing their sins and were being baptized (3:6). Even the false teachers in Matthew's church and the Pharisees and Sadducees at the time of John and Jesus were capable of a public display of remorse, as John still demands from them fruits to show their repentant condition (3:8)" (253–54).

[21] Douglas D. Webster, *Selling Jesus: What's Wrong with Marketing the Church* (Downers Grove, Ill.: InterVarsity, 1992), 119.

[22] Church Growth Study Committee, *Christ's Commission*, 4.

[23] George Barna and Mark Hatch, *Boiling Point: It Only Takes One Degree; Monitoring Cultural Shifts in the 21st Century* (Ventura, Calif.: Gospel Light/Regal Books, 2001), 236 (used by permission). Barna goes on to show that even with all the innovative tactics of CG, e.g., megachurches and small groups, the results are not encouraging. Average attendance at worship went from an average of 99 adults on a weekend in 1990 to only 90 in the year 2000.

[24] Luecke, *Apostolic Style*, 20.

[25] Ibid., 21.

CHAPTER 6

[1] Hunter, *Confessions*, 220.

[2] Marquart, "'CG' as Mission Paradigm," 153.

[3] Roland Cap Heike, *Proverbs: People's Bible* (Milwaukee: Northwestern, 1992), 291–92.

[4] Hunter, *Confessions*: "These are congregational communities without a dream, without a vision, without a goal, and, therefore, without any strategy for outreach. The fact is that many of these congregations have little evangelism, meet few needs beyond the community of believers, and are involved in very little to reach out to unchurched neighbors and friends—except at the time of the annual bazaar, when they invite them to come in so that they can get their money to pay for the maintenance of the institution" (221).

[5] For a source on marketing applied to the church, see George Barna, *A Step-by-Step Guide to Church Marketing* (Ventura, Calif.: Gospel Light/Regal Books, 1992). For those interested in the principles of marketing as taught to first-year business students in colleges and universities, see the textbook by E. Jerome McCarthy cited in the introduction.

[6] Barna, *A Step-by-Step Guide*, 22.

[7] Stephen D. Hower, *Sharpening the Sword: A Call to Strong and Courageous Leadership* (St. Louis: Concordia Publishing House, 1996), 4–5.

[8] Heinecke, et al., *Courageous Churches*, 90.

[9] Spencer Johnson, *Who Moved My Cheese?* (New York: G. P. Putnam, 1998).

[10] Heinecke, et al., *Courageous Churches*: "In summary, while the shepherd image continues to be a viable and favorite model among pastors and church leaders, and is strongly fostered in theological education because of the biblical imagery, it inherently is oriented to preservation of the flock by the Shepherd. In most of the cases we studied, leadership holds out a mission vision and brings about appropriate changes to accomplish mission tasks. Strong pastoral leadership, especially in larger churches, consciously limits personal shepherding to staff and key leaders and their families and places more time on visioning, communicating, coordinating relationships, and the overall mission of the congregation. The sheep are expected to care for and to produce more sheep" (106). In an amazing reversal of the desire to "please people," this CG orientation at times supports disenchanting those members (sheep) who don't go along with the new marketing orientation: "A test of leadership styles comes when opposition to the mission arises. In almost every case in this study, a few and sometimes many members became unhappy with their church's new

direction. Believing that support orientation tends to set aside the trouble-causing goal so that peace can be restored and, thereby, allow growth to level off, these task/mission-oriented ministers keep pulling—even in the face of opposition. The external mission of outreach seems more important than some unhappy members" (105).

11 Brown-Driver-Briggs-Gesenius, *Hebrew and English Lexicon* (1979 reprint by Christian Copyrights), 303a.3. Keil-Delitzsch, *Commentary on the Old Testament*, vol. 6 (Grand Rapids, Mich.: Eerdmans, 1982): "'Chazon' is according to the sense, equivalent to 'gebuaah,' the prophetic revelation in itself, and as the contents of that which is proclaimed. Without spiritual preaching, proceeding from spiritual experience, a people is unrestrained; it becomes disorderly, Ex. 32:25; *wild und wust,* as Luther translates" (252). Lutheran OT scholar Paul Raabe devotes a good deal of attention to this word in his excellent Obadiah commentary: "What is the precise meaning of 'chazon'? Does it denote the act of seeing, the event in which a divine revelation comes, or the content of the prophetic message itself? It is never used as a verbal noun to denote the act of seeing, and in only one passage does it designate the event or subjective experience in which a divine message comes to the recipient, Ps. 89:20(19). . . . In all the other passages the noun designates the content of the prophetic revelation, the message itself" (*Obadiah: A New Translation with Introduction and Commentary*, Anchor Bible, vol. 24D [New York: Doubleday, 1996], 94–96). The recognized Old Testament wisdom scholar Derek Kidner concurs: "Vision (AV,RV) is to be taken in its exact sense of the revelation a prophet receives. Law in line 2 is its complement. 'The law, the prophets and the wisdom literature meet in this verse' (*The New Bible Commentary*). Perish (AV): rather, 'run wild.' The verb means to let loose, e.g. to let one's hair down" (*Proverbs: An Introduction and Commentary*, Tyndale Old Testament Commentaries [Downers Grove, Ill.: Tyndale, 1964], 175–76).

12 The NIV Bible translates as such.

13 See also Keil-Delitzsch in n. 11, where it is translated as "unrestrained" or "disorderly." Also note that Kidner translates as "run wild" rather than "perish."

14 See, for example, their misunderstanding and misapplication of "adiaphora," in the excellent article by Matthew Harrison, "Martin Chemnitz."

15 Church Growth Study Committee, *Christ's Commission*, 2.

16 Phillip D. Kenneson and James L. Street, *Selling Out the Church: The Dangers of Church Marketing* (Nashville: Abingdon, 1997), 16 (used by permission).

[17] Ibid., 17: "We believe that many Christians and non-Christians alike are understandably confused about the purpose of Christ's church. As we will see, one of the claimed benefits of church marketing is a clearer vision of the church's mission. Although we do not want to deny that this could happen, we do worry that the image of the church that marketing philosophy presupposes and the kind of church that marketing practice helps to create are seriously distorted." In the foreword, Stanley Hauerwas makes this pertinent observation: "Kenneson and Street help us see that the marketer's presumption that form can be separated from the content of the gospel betrays an understanding of the gospel that cannot help betraying the gift that is Christ" (11).

[18] A. L. Barry, "Doctrine and Evangelism: Always Both/And, Never Either/Or!" *Concordia Theological Quarterly* 65 (Jan. 2001), 4.

[19] Ibid., 7.

[20] Ibid., 11. Compare with CG spokesmen usage of Acts 15: "The Apostolic Convention is pivotal for the understanding of congregations joined together in a larger unity. . . . I [have] described how the apostles very carefully distinguished between substance and style in order to set boundaries for churches to consider themselves part of the Christian movement" (Luecke, *Apostolic Style*, 106).

[21] Barry, "Doctrine and Evangelism": "Where this single article remains pure, Christendom will remain pure, in beautiful harmony, and without any schisms. But where it does not remain pure, it is impossible to repel any error or heretical spirit" (11).

[22] Ibid., 12.

CHAPTER 7

[1] Hunter, *Confessions*, 205–06.

[2] Luecke, *Apostolic Style*, 11.

[3] A. L. Barry, "Challenges in Church and Ministry in the LCMS," *Church and Ministry: The Collected Papers of the 150th Anniversary Theological Convocation of the LCMS* (St. Louis: Office of the President, LCMS, 1998), 3–4, 6.

[4] Marquart, "'CG' as Mission Paradigm," 83.

[5] Church Growth Study Committee, *Christ's Commission*, 3.

[6] Barry, "Challenges," 77.

[7] Hunter, *Confessions*, 209.

[8] Ibid., 199.

[9] Ibid., 201.

[10] Marquart, "'CG' as Mission Paradigm," 82.

[11] Ibid.

[12] Ibid., 82–83.

[13] Ibid., 84.

[14] Barry, "Challenges," 102.

[15] See Marquart, "'CG' as Mission Paradigm," 52–54, 59–64, 69–75. Commenting on non-Lutheran CG expert Carl George's comment that the pastor is the Chief Executive Officer who casts the vision, which then rightly places the ministry where it belongs, with laypeople, Marquart writes: "Perfect sense though all this makes from a Pentecostal point of view, one can hardly imagine anything more diametrically opposed to the biblical, Lutheran preaching and sacraments orientation. Yet instead of warning against the book's seductions, much of our Synod's official 'missions' and 'evangelism' leadership zealously distributes it and advocates its 'mega-church' message! No more substantive correctives appear to be offered than a sprinkling of ritual incantations about 'Word and Sacrament'! There is no hint of an inkling of just how contrary this 'paradigm' is to our Confession's whole understanding of the Gospel" (80–81).

[16] Kurt Marquart, "Response to Presentation II," quoted in Barry, "Challenges," 104.

[17] Ibid.

[18] Ibid., 109. Here Marquart quotes Rom. 10:15: "How shall they preach unless they are sent?"

[19] Marquart, "'CG' as Mission Paradigm," 61. This is his assessment of the consistent heart of McGavran's theology and, thus, CG's theology.

[20] Luecke, *Apostolic Style*, 121.

[21] Hunter, *Confessions*, 199.

[22] Ibid., 199–216.

[23] Ibid., 199–200.

[24] Luecke, *Apostolic Style*, 112–13.

[25] Ibid., 116–17.

[26] Ibid., 115. He quotes from James Pragman's book that Gerhard provided the false doctrine that there is a divinely instituted office of the means of grace. The important implication is that all other ministry is only derivative from the one ordained, divinely instituted office.

[27] Ibid., 111. "The issue is what to call the congregational leader who

preaches, administers the sacraments, and is responsible for the spiritual dimension of church life. . . . In Missouri Synod translations, *Predigtamt* came out of the Office of Public Ministry, often shortened to Public Ministry. Much has changed in the translation. What is 'public ministry,' and where do you find this position in Scripture?" For the failure to follow the apostle Paul's ministry principles, see page 117 of Luecke's book.

[28] Hunter, *Confessions*, 210.

[29] Luecke, *Apostolic Style*, 118.

[30] Hunter, *Confessions*, 210.

[31] Ibid., 211.

[32] Ibid., 212.

[33] Marquart, "'CG' as Mission Paradigm," 89.

[34] Ibid., 96–97.

[35] Ibid., 57.

[36] Preus, "Review of *Confessions of a CG Enthusiast*," 50.

[37] Ibid., 51. Preus explains: "Such churches experience 'the essence of grace' when they rid themselves of empty traditions and break down cultural barriers of those who are receptive to God. In 'missionary-thinking' churches, the clergy inspire and encourage while the ministers, that is, all Christians, take up the vocation of pastor. Unity in the Church Growth Movement is based not on a common confession of the doctrine of the gospel, but on a common acceptance of the church-growth paradigm. All articles of faith are measured against the movement's understanding of the 'great commission.'"

[38] Henry P. Hamann, "The Translation of Ephesians 4:12—A Necessary Revision," *Concordia Journal*, vol. 10 (Jan. 1988), 42.

[39] Ibid., 46. Hamann continues: "Certainly the needs of the laymen saints are cared for: they receive salvation, eternal life, ethical instructions through the saving word, the seal of the sacraments, the doctrinal decisions, the disciplinary measures administered by the officers. Yet two implications of this interpretation are inescapable: (1) the laymen are ultimately only beneficiaries, and (2) the benefits of the clergy's work remain inside the church—though people and powers outside the church may witness the clergy's successes and failures."

[40] Ibid., 48. I have paraphrased Hamann's comments here. He includes a host of scriptural references: Acts 2:42–47; 20:7–11; 1 Cor. 11:14; 16:2; Heb. 10:25; 1 Tim. 2:1–8; 3:1–7; 4:9–10; Titus 1:5–9; 2:3–5; James 5:14; Acts 20:28; Heb. 13:17; 1 Pet 4:11; 5:1–4.

[41] Ibid., 49.

CHAPTER 8

[1] Luecke, *Apostolic Style*, 33.

[2] Ibid., 99.

[3] Hunter, *Confessions*, 23.

[4] Preus, "Review of *Confessions of a CG Enthusiast*," 46, 51.

[5] Marquart, "'CG' as Mission Paradigm," 70.

[6] Hunter, *Confessions*, 23.

[7] Ibid., 190.

[8] Luecke, *Apostolic Style*, 13.

[9] Hunter, *Confessions*, 29.

[10] Luecke, *Apostolic Style*, 13.

[11] Marquart, "'CG' as Mission Paradigm," 71.

[12] Ibid., 72.

[13] Ibid., 72.

[14] Hunter, *Confessions*, 36–39.

[15] Ibid., 37.

[16] See Luecke, *Apostolic Style*, 89–98, and Hunter, *Confessions*, 107–11. The following remarks from Hunter are relevant to the previous discussion about Dr. Cho's Pentecostal belief in prayer as a means of grace: "Paul Yonggi Cho is pastor of the largest church in the world in Seoul, Korea. On numerous occasions I have had other opportunity to speak with Dr. Cho at his church, the Yoido Full Gospel Church. Each time that I have seen him I have asked him the question, 'What would you say is the secret of the growth of this, the largest church in Christian history?' Over the years, his answer has been consistent. He could talk about the cell group ministry, the structure of the church, or its programs and ministries. He could talk about his own leadership qualities. He could even discuss the receptivity of the South Korean people. But his answer is always short and to the point: 'The reason for the growth of this church is that God answers prayer. We are serious about prayer'" (108).

[17] Hunter, *Confessions*, 111.

[18] Jeffrey J. Kloha and Ronald R. Feuerhahn, eds., *Scripture and the Church: Selected Essays of Herman Sasse* (St. Louis: Concordia Seminary, 1995), 214. For a wonderful look at the life and theology of this man, see also John R. Stephenson and Thomas M. Winger, eds., *Herman Sasse: A Man for Our Times?* (St. Louis: Concordia Publishing House, 1998).

[19] Ibid., 205.

[20] Ibid., 203.

[21] Ibid., 219.

[22] Marquart, "'CG' as Mission Paradigm," 71.

[23] Ibid., 64.

[24] Luecke, *Apostolic Style*, 67.

[25] Ibid., 67.

[26] Ibid., 28ff.

[27] Ibid., 28.

[28] Ibid., 28–29.

[29] 1998 Resolution 3-05, "To Reaffirm Our Practice of Admission to the Lord's Supper," *LCMS Convention Proceedings*, 115.

[30] Hunter, *Confessions*, 237.

[31] Luecke, *Apostolic Style*, 68–69.

[32] Church Growth Study Commitee, *Christ's Commission*, 4: "Therefore, it is spiritual harmful when a generic Christianity downplays controversial biblical truths in favor of a least-common denominator approach to doctrine, practice, and fellowship, thus compromising Christ's mission on earth. (*Formula of Concord* SD X, 5–7)."

[33] 1995 Concordia Theological Symposium Banquet.

CHAPTER 9

[1] Hunter, *Confessions*, 183–84.

[2] Church Growth Study Committee, *Christ's Commission*, 2.

[3] Ibid., 6.

[4] Barry, "Doctrine and Evangelism," 3–4.

[5] Ibid., 13.

[6] Church Growth Study Committee, *Christ's Commission*, 7.

[7] Ibid.

[8] Ibid.

[9] Hunter, *Confessions*, 174. I must add that the context for this quote is not one Confessionalists can support. For example, Hunter states: "Even discipling, at its best, takes place in a mentoring process beyond the walls of a church building" (174). This is totally opposed to the Lutheran understanding of the Office of the Public Ministry as a gift from Christ (Eph. 4:11 controversy). See also Romans 10:14. The true teaching about the priesthood of all believers is that they take Christ to those in their life streams.

[10] Ibid., 182.

[11] Barry, "Doctrine and Evangelism," 4.

[12] Ibid., 7.

[13] A. L. Barry, "The President's Report to the 60th Regular Convention of The Lutheran Church—Missouri Synod," Part III, 8, 9.

[14] Ibid., 7.

[15] Ibid., 10.

[16] Hunter, *Confessions*, 184.

[17] Ibid.

[18] Ibid., 185.

[19] Barry, "Doctrine and Evangelism," 11.

[20] Ibid., 4.

[21] D. A. Carson, *The Gagging of God: Christianity Confronts Pluralism* (Grand Rapids, Mich.: Zondervan, 1996), 477 (used by permission). He also makes this point about audience sovereignty in relation to cultural changes: "Although we must communicate the gospel in categories that are not in the first instance alien to the people we are addressing, our whole aim must be to get them to think and know God in the categories that he has himself provided. Our analysis of human needs must be based on the Bible's identification of human needs, even if it is necessary to show how the Bible's presentation of human need is connected, often in ways they did not expect, to the ways human beings define their own needs. Otherwise, the gospel itself will always get perverted with time. This stance, surely, is reflected in apostolic terms of ministry."

[22] Michael Ruhlman (New York: Viking, 2000).

[23] In a previous theological era, for Lutherans "traditional" meant the time period around 1580.

CHAPTER 10

[1] Luecke, *Apostolic Style*, 109.

[2] Ibid., 100.

[3] Ibid., 47.

[4] Hunter, *Confessions*, 144.

[5] Ibid., 247–48.

[6] Kurt A. Marquart, "The Church in the Twenty-First Century: Will There Be a Lutheran One?" in Dean Wenthe, et al., eds., *All Theology Is Christology: Essays in Honor of David P. Scaer* (Ft. Wayne, Ind.: Concordia Theological Seminary, 2000), 181–83.

[7] Church Growth Study Committee, *Christ's Commission*, 7.

[8] A. L. Barry, *What Does This Mean? Catechesis in the Lutheran Congregation* (St. Louis: Office of the President, LCMS, 1996), 1–2.

[9] Ibid., 72.

[10] Hunter, *Confessions*, 187.

[11] Marquart, "'CG' as Mission Paradigm," 168.

[12] Luecke, *Apostolic Style*, 109.

[13] Ibid.

[14] Ibid., 109–10.

[15] Marquart, "The Church in the Twenty-First Century," 183.

[16] Ibid., 190.

[17] Ibid., 190–91.

[18] Ibid., 193.

[19] Ibid., 196–97.

[20] David Buegler, "Three Trends Cannot Be Stopped," *Jesus First* 17 (Mar. 2001), 8.

[21] Marquart, "The Church in the Twenty-First Century," 185–86.

[22] Ibid., 144. For Hunter's charge that the Lutheran church has "undermined the essence of the incarnation," see Klemet Preus's excellent analysis of this strange notion and its background theology in his review of *Confessions of a Church Growth Enthusiast*, where he examines Hunter's Christology. Preus charges Hunter with an unbiblical and unlutheran view of the theology of the cross: "He is forced to define the cross in terms of the great commission rather than the great commission in terms of the cross. No longer does the cross inform us that disciples are made by baptizing into the death of Christ and teaching the doctrine of the blood atonement. Rather, the great commission informs us that 'we are in partnership with God,' because of 'the multiplication that comes about through His death and resurrection. It moves the mission of God from the one (Jesus) to the many (His disciples).' The suffering and death of Jesus serve the great commission. And that is the essence of the Church Growth Movement. What is incarnational ministry to Hunter? 'The desire to let the Gospel get through to the target audience with the least amount of resistance is nothing other than the desire for incarnational ministry'" (47).

[23] Robert D. Preus and Wilbert H. Rosin, *A Contemporary Look at the Formula of Concord* (St. Louis: Concordia Publishing House, 1978), 9, 10.

[24] Conflated from a presentation by Dr. J. A. O. Preus, Jr., entitled "Chem-

nitz and Controversy," given at Concordia Seminary, St. Louis, on November 5, 1986, and from his book *The Second Martin: The Life and Theology of Martin Chemnitz* (St. Louis: Concordia Publishing House, 1994).